Toxic Rel

A Step-by-Step Guide With Tactics And Conversation Skills

Around Difficult People With Toxic Personalities

Luke F. Gregory © 2016

Legal Disclaimer

Table of Contents

Welcome to the Real World

Life is the most precious gift that we will ever have. Life is beautiful and exciting and enjoyable. How you choose to live is up to you. However, let's face it, navigating the real world can suck sometimes. The real world is not always as beautiful and exciting and enjoyable, and we wish it would be.

There is nothing wrong with getting a little bit of advice from time to time on what you can do to make the journey of life a bit easier. That is where this book comes in. I am here to help you manage something that everyone will deal with at some point in their life: toxic people.

What exactly do you mean by "Toxic"?

Before I can go any further, we have a few things that we have to get out of the way first. There are a lot of ways to define a toxic person for the simple fact that there are so many different types of toxic people out there. We will begin by starting with a practical definition that covers all of the variations: a toxic person is someone who has the potential to impact both you and your livelihood negatively.

Ultimately, a toxic person is bad for you. The reason that a toxic person is so dangerous is that often they are not readily recognized as being very toxic. You could go days, months, or even years associating with these types of people and never even know how much damage that they are causing in your life. It can be very stressful to not be able to decipher between who is really trying to be a positive influence in your life and who isn't.

Luckily, this is where this book will be most helpful. To protect yourself from a toxic person, you have to be able to know one when you see one. There are always signs; just be able to identify them. The next few chapters will be dedicated to doing just that: telling you about the different types of toxic people that are out there, and then giving you some tips on what you can do to either develop a healthy relationship with them or to get rid of them altogether. Get ready. I'm sure that some of these descriptions will open your eyes to the types of people that are wreaking havoc on your happiness.

Disclaimer

The characterizations that you are about to read describe types of toxic people. It will be beneficial for you to keep in mind that there is no cookie-cutter personality or type of person or type of toxicity. In fact, you will most likely have to examine your life and the people that influence you, to see if anyone has traces of these traits. If they do, you will have to decide if it's a low enough toxicity to deal with (as we all have our own personal weaknesses, problems, and flaws) or if they're poisoning your life.

Additionally, these are generalizations. Hence, I ask that no one is offended if you find that a certain trait sounds like it might describe you. Take heart! If it does, in fact, represent you, you now know what to work on. If it somewhat describes you, you probably have a healthy personality, and while you may lean towards one of these types during moments of weakness, you lean away from them in times of strength. You're on the right track. If you don't think you have any personal traces of toxicity at all, that may be all well and good, but it might be worth asking a close friend or loved one what they think about you. The rest of this book is about clearing your life of toxic people – just make sure you're not toxic to the people that you interact with on a regular basis.

Lastly, it is highly recommended that you remove toxic people from your life. As already stated, it is up to you if you do so, and it is up to you who qualifies as "toxic" in your life; as you read the following chapters, you will automatically think of people in your life who qualify. Don't discount that gut feeling. I know a friend who recently had to cut out a couple of family members from her life. It was not easy, fast, or painless, but she did it, and she has a happier life now because of it. She had to endure people giving her a hard time about it, but as time passed, everyone else around her could tell that she had made the right decision. Trust your judgment; you know who is putting life into you and who is sucking it out of you. Don't let other suck your life out of you.

This book will help you understand types of toxic people, how to deal with them, and how to decide if you should remove them from your life. It will give you practical tips to deal with the different toxic people that may be in your life and encouraging phrases, to sum up, each chapter. At the end of the day, you are the one who has to decide and stand by that decision. You can do it! You deserve a good life, void of toxicity.

"You don't ever have to feel guilty about removing toxic people from your life. It doesn't matter whether someone is a relative, romantic interest, employer, a childhood friend, or a new acquaintance – you don't have to make room for people who cause you pain or make you feel small. It's one thing if a person owns up to their behavior and makes an effort to change. But if a person disregards your feelings, ignore your boundaries, and 'continues' to treat you in a harmful way, they need to go."

-Daniell Koepke

The "Look-at-Me-er"

Anna is one of the hardest working people around. She's been a supervisor at the bank for over ten years and is beloved by her customers. Many hours of her day are spent trying to educate herself about her job so that she can continue to be valuable to her clients. The people that she works with notice her valiant efforts, and regularly applaud her for her ability to continuously make everyone happy.

Despite Anna's success at her job, her personal life is in shackles. Because of her hard work ethic in the workplace, she barely makes time for her husband. As a result, he eventually divorced her and took everything that she owned. Because of lack of resources, she was forced to move back in with her parents. Anna has a younger sister named Julie, who had only one goal: marry a rich guy. She regularly wore provocative clothing and put on tons of makeup in hopes of catching the eye of an eligible bachelor.

After years of putting herself out there, she finally found the type of man she was looking for. Every chance she got, she expressed her happiness to Anna. Her expressed happiness came across as what most people would consider gloating. Since her boyfriend was rich, Julie constantly received new clothes, jewelry, and even a new car. She always flashed her jewelry in Anna's face and bragged about how great her life was, prancing around in her designer clothing and acting like she is the center of the universe.

When Anna would tell her how bad her day was, Julie replied by saying how great her day was as opposed to being empathetic towards her sister. When Anna would try to explain something to her sister about her day, Julie would interrupt her and go on a tangent about everything that her new boyfriend was doing for her. Julie was completely self-centered and had no interest in anyone else's life unless she could find a way to incorporate her own life into the story. It got to the point to where nothing Anna said mattered to Julie because all Julie wanted to do was tell everyone the expensive items that she was getting from her boyfriend.

Psychoanalysis:

Behind the selfish, self-centered outer layer of the Look-At-Me-er is a weak and self-conscious core. They desire to be approved of; they want to be liked. As an adult, you may wonder why such a person is so self-centered and unwilling to talk about anyone or anything outside of him or herself. His or her brain has been hard-wired to protect him or herself and provide happiness for him or herself.

This most likely comes from the events of their childhood (As you continue reading, you will find that all toxic people most likely can link their traits to their past. This is cause for empathy, but not cause for compliance.). A Look-At-Me-er may not have gotten the attention they desired as a child or may have found that the only way to earn love is to be flashy, loud, and self-absorbed. Let's imagine Anna and Julie's childhood. Anna, being the first-born, got a good amount of love and attention from their parents. Once Julie was born, though, life got busier for the family, and though their parents tried to show equal love and attention to both girls, Julie felt like she wasn't loved as much as Anna. This may only be because their family had more to do and less time to spend solely on Julie. However, Julie may have found that the best way to get the love and attention that she desired was by forcing it. She learned to interrupt Anna to show mom and dad *her* project from school. She learned to be loud, flashy, and aggressive. She focused on herself so that other people would, too – all in the search to feel loved and accepted.

We all have childhoods that have somehow shaped us. However, the Look-At-Me-er has allowed his or her childhood to shape he or her into a self-centered person. The Look-At-Me-er wants to be in the spotlight and doesn't naturally think about the needs and desires of others, even those that they profess to care about.

What's the problem?

Anna's sister is what we will call a Look At Me-er. A Look At Me-er is a person that is hopelessly self-centered and always finds a way to make things about them. A Look At Me-er is colloquially known as a Show-off. Although they do not seem dangerous, they have a lot more impact on your life than you realize.

The most significant impact is on your self-esteem. Constantly having someone gloat and talk about himself or herself when you are in a low place directly correlates to an unhealthy self-concept. You will find yourself comparing your life to theirs, being envious of what they have, and even second-guessing whether or not your life is worthwhile. It's crucial to protect yourself from these types of people, and the following tips can help you do just that.

Tell them about themselves.

This is probably the most important thing you can do to this type of person. The majority of the time, the Look At Me-er does not even realize that he or she is gloating. They see nothing wrong with talking about themselves all the time, so they just continue to do it. Typically, this results from having low self-esteem themselves. They use the gloating as a way to compensate for what they believe is missing from their lives.

In other words, it's a defense mechanism to help them feel better about their own insecurities. Be honest with them, and kindly but firmly let them know that they are selfish. You would be surprised at how quickly this could solve the problem. In fact, you may even be able to steer them away from their selfish attitude.

Interrupt them back.

This may seem rude, but it is a very effective way to get the point across. Sometimes, the person will know that they are a Look At Me-er and not care. If that person isn't your friend and you have no choice but to interact with them, then it is time for you to start being assertive. If they start to interrupt you while you're trying to talk, return the favor. Interrupt them back and divert the attention away from them. If you do it the right way (assertively, but not rudely), they will catch the hint and respect you by shutting up.

Ignore them.

Although not usually the first choice if you're a nice person, ignoring them is also very effective. Think of it like this: remember when you were growing up, how you had a class clown who always told jokes at the wrong times? Well, it is a well-known fact that the class clown will stop clowning if he does not have an audience. The same can be said about the Look At Me-er. If there no one to listen to them boast, then he or she will stop talking. Never forget: Look At Me-ers love an audience. They thrive on the attention. If you stop giving them attention, then they will stop bragging. It's as simple as that.

Conversing with A Look-At-Me-er:

When you do engage with a Look-At-Me-er, you can tweak your conversation style to make it easier on yourself. How, when all they want to do is talk about them? Here are a couple of suggestions.

First - Give them time to share. If you know someone is self-centered and is only going to keep drawing the conversation back to them, let them have some time in the limelight. Ask them about themselves, and actively listen to them. This isn't the only tactic that you should use, though. If you are only always listening to them, then you aren't sharing in a real conversation.

Second - Respond with confidence. If you have something to contribute, do so with an aggressive and assertive voice. Let them know that you can equally contribute to the conversation. This can open the door to you sharing your own life instead of only listening to them brag about theirs. Show your value and your credentials. If you've been through something that relates to what they are talking about, be confident that it matters, and don't let them interrupt you to keep talking about themselves. Tell them, "Let me finish, and then I'd love to hear what you want to share."

Third - Use their trait against them. If you want to share something with them, or want their advice about something, let them know this by asking them. You could say something like this: "I know you've been through something like this before, can you hear me out and then let me know what you think I should do?" Little by little, this tactic may help to even out the playing field. You are showing them that they have value, without de-valuing yourself. Hopefully, you can create a friendship where two-way sharing happens.

Approaching Conflict - In order to approach conflict and have a peaceful confrontation with a Look-At-Me-er, here are some helpful tips:

- Remember that they want to turn the conversation back to them. Tell them that you need to discuss something with them. Keep it short so that they won't lose interest and try to change the subject. Don't go into a long compliant about how he isn't a good friend. Don't yell at her. The Look-At-Me-er doesn't respond well in those situations. Concisely confront him in a kind way.

- Acknowledge what they are doing right. Look-At-Me-ers hate being told that they have done something wrong. It makes them look bad, and that is their least favorite thing. Be ready to point out a good example of when they did stop and listen to you, and share with them the positive way it made you feel.

- Give them an easy step to fix the problem. If you need to confront him or her about something that needs to change – for example, he or she is always rudely cutting you off in meetings to share his or her ideas – give him or her a practical step to focus on that will alleviate the problem. For instance, tell him or her to focus on waiting until you are done talking to share. All he or she has to do it save their comment until there is an opening in the conversation to share.

While these simple tactics can help, if your Look-At-Me-er friend is too toxic, even conversation aids will not help, and you may want to consider if you really have a deep friendship with this person.

Wrap Up

If they are toxic to your life and growth, there is a very high probability that you need to either distance yourself from them or use one of the tips to manage the relationship. As a quick recap, here are some of the signs that you are dealing with a Look At Me-er:

- Talks excessively about the things that they have
- Strives to get everyone's attention
- Has no concern over for what anyone else has going on

"Life is too short to spend time with people who suck the happiness out of you."

-YourTango.com

The Debbie Downer

Rachel is part of a small group of friends. Rachel is the most outgoing; she is always finding new adventures for her clique to try. Whether it's climbing a mountain, hiking a nature trail, or even just going to see a movie, Rachel is chalked full of ideas. Although most of her friends are up for whatever Rachel chooses, one of the girls in her group, Joyce, is the exact opposite.

Joyce has a pessimistic attitude. In other words, she tends to look at the bad side of everything instead of the good side. For example, when Rachel suggests climbing the mountain, Joyce will reply by saying how there's no point because you have to climb back down anyway. No good will come from hiking a nature trail because you will spend more time fighting off bugs than enjoying the hike. She even says that they shouldn't go to a movie because critics said it was bad, and they would be better off waiting for it to come out on DVD.

Joyce's negative attitude caused a wedge in the group – every time they tried to have fun, Joyce would find a way to make things look like a drag. She always complains about everything that they do and never seems to want anyone to have a good time.

Psychoanalysis:

Debbie Downers not only have negative feelings now and then, but they are also chronically negative. The way that their brain is wired, they focus on the negative about small things because they want to be able to control them. They feel safer when there aren't unknowns that they can't control. Debbie Downers feel better focusing on being negative and pessimistic on the present, and the future as well, so that they don't have to think about past events that may have influenced them.

Debbie Downers can be harmful due to past injuries – whether physical, emotional, mental, or spiritual. Let's imagine Joyce as a young child. She was happy and free-spirited, but her mom was always nagging on her to be careful. Whenever something bad would happen, even something small, Joyce's mom would make comments like, "see, that's what happens when you're too adventurous" or "I warned you to be careful and you didn't listen and now you've gotten hurt" or even a simple "I told you so". Additionally, Joyce's dad left her mom for another woman. Joyce couldn't understand it. All she learned is that bad things happen in life, and you should guard yourself against pretty much anything.

Those memories have rewired Joyce's brain to protect her from incurring pain in any way in adulthood. She sees the bad in everything and struggles to be positive. Personally, she doesn't think she's good enough, or she thinks she's too much, and so she assumes the worst about everything. The more that you think a thought, the more solidified it becomes in your mind, and the more it affects how you behave. While Debbie Downers have wired their brains to be negative, it is not your fault that they've done that, and it does not fall on you to fix them or to suffer through their toxicity. They need to work on improving themselves through self-help books, positivity practice, and possibly professional counseling.

What's the problem?

Joyce is what many people call a Debbie Downer. They always play down everything good that happens to make it seem as if it is unimportant, boring, or threatening. Essentially, they are the type of people who cannot take any positive words or compliments and instead find ways to make the situation negative.

The dangerous thing about a Debbie Downer is that often their attitudes can be contagious. If you are constantly around someone who is pessimistic or unhappy, it is just a matter of time before that negative energy will rub off on you. Before you know it, you will find yourself looking at the bad side of things too.

Be proactive, and get away from this type of person as soon as possible. Debbie Downers tend to experience high levels of stress and therefore exert that stress on others. You don't want to be a Debbie Downer. If you find yourself around one, here are some tips to help alleviate the situation.

Kill them with kindness.

This is the most important thing you can do when dealing with a Debbie Downer. Just like the Look At Me-er, the Debbie Downer likes an audience as well. They need an audience for a slightly different reason: to gain support. In other words, they are looking for people to be negative about them. The phrase "misery loves company" plays a significant role in this situation. Don't allow yourself to be lured into that trap.

Keep yourself positive, and combat the Debbie Downer's negative attitude with an upbeat attitude. For example, if Joyce said something about having to fight bugs when they went on a hike, Rachel could simply suggest that they bring lots of bug spray or wear long sleeves and pants. The trick is to interject their interjection by keeping the atmosphere positive. As long as you stay optimistic, you will not become as miserable as a Debbie Downer, and you may alter their attitude through your good example.

Ignore them.

Ignoring a Debbie Downer is different from ignoring the Look At Me-er. In this case, you ignore them by continuing the conversation as if they never said anything. It's not rude. Instead, think of it as your way of subtly suggesting that you will not allow their negative attitude to change the conversation. If everyone ignores the Debbie Downer, then (like the class clown) they will not say anything else about it. This only works if the Debbie Downer is not persistent. If they are persistent, then revert to the previous tip.

Cheer them up.

This may be a bit of a stretch for the super Debbie Downer, but it is worth a shot. Remember that Debbie Downers are typically very depressed people. One of the reasons that people get depressed is because they do not have friends around that can make them happy. Another reason is that they are overly anxious about the details of situations and can only see the negative outcomes. Take the time to talk to your Debbie Downer and see what it is that has made them so pessimistic. Then, find a way to get them out of the mind frame that everything is bad. Once you cheer them up and get them out of that negative mindset, they will be a lot more pleasant to be around.

Conversing with a Debbie Downer

Debbie Downers are negative people. If you're not careful, you will easily find yourself slipping into the negative language of the Debbie Downer. You have to focus on remaining positive in their presence. In order to converse with them, you will want to consider using some of the following tactics.

First - Determine that you will remain positive despite their attitude, and let it show through your words. For example, if you are with Joyce, and she is complaining about the rainy weather, you could join her, or you could say something like this: "I don't mind the rain at all, it's the perfect day to stay in and watch a movie."

Second - Validate their feelings. Recognize what they are feeling, and then show them a better way to feel. If you are at work and have a Debbie Downer complaining about how terrible everything is, it's ok to validate their feelings first. Let them know that you understand where they are coming from, or that you see how they could be feeling that way. Then, use your words to speak some positivity to them (and to keep yourself from the downward spiral of negative talk).

Say something like this: "It is not a fun project, that's for sure. I think we can handle it, though!" Be encouraging and positive. Show Debbie Downer that there is another way to act, speak, and feel. They will appreciate that you validated their feelings, and will be more open to altering their behavior.

Third - Be optimistically realistic. There's no use in being positive to the point that you're not even realistic. If something bad has happened, it is ok to express negative emotions. You shouldn't ignore what your friends are feeling. Let your Debbie Downer express complaint or frustration if it is warranted. Choose to respond with optimistic reality.

For example, if you and your friends are out on a hike, and your Debbie Downer friend is anxious that she will pull a muscle like she did last time, you can address her with a mix of optimism and reality. Say something like this: "that is a possibility, but we can take actions against that happening. Let's stretch before we start, and pay attention to our path and pace as we go! Let me know if you need a rest!" Work with them, if you can, and show them that you can help alleviate their worry and negativity.

Approaching Conflict - If you are free-spirited, positive, or even just an average human being, you will run into conflict if you have some kind of relationship with a Debbie Downer. How can you confront them peacefully? Here are some practical ways to work through conflict with such a person.

- Start with a positive comment. When you are getting ready to talk about a potentially negative subject with a negative person, start out with something positive. This will hopefully relax them a little bit, and allow them to open up and hear what you have to say.

- Tell them the truth, and offer help. This does not mean you take on their problem. If they are a negative influence in your life, and you're trying to tell them that, offer them a way to get better and offer your support. Don't just tell them that they are super negative and expect them to accept that and change. If you need to confront them about how they are talking and behaving, offer them a suggestion on how they can improve. This helps especially in the workplace. If a Debbie Downer is creating conflict and you need it to change, suggest a book that you know of that works on people skills or positive thinking. There are tons out there that can help chronically negative people to work on their character.

- End with a positive comment. Debbie Downers need you to be gentle with them, or all that they will take away from a confrontation is everything that is bad and everything that they are doing wrong. In fact, they will hear things that they've done wrong that is nowhere in what you said to them. Encourage them that they are a good friend or a good employee and that you know they have the ability to improve and succeed.

Wrap Up

These tactics can help you in speaking to a Debbie Downer. They are not bad people to be around if they are changeable; however, some Debbie Downers are stuck in their ways and refuse to be helped. These are tougher – nearly impossible – to reason with. Here are the fundamental signs of a Debbie Downer:

- Always thinks that the worst possible thing can and will happen
- Hesitates to doing anything fun or out of the box

- All-around negative person

"Don't let bitter, unhappy people drag you down to their level. Instead, use their behavior as an example of how not to behave and be grateful you are nothing like them."

-Heartfelt Quotes

The Rebellious Soul

Greg is the type of person who always follows the rules. He goes to work, goes to school, and tends to stay out of trouble. Even though he is a good guy, Greg still manages to find himself in awkward situations, which are the result of hanging out with his friend Bobby. Bobby is a very exciting person to be around. He enjoys doing things that are completely out of the box, and that tend to be questionable. Although things usually end up okay, there are times when Greg questions Bobby's intentions.

Yes, Bobby is a very "cool" person; however, his exciting ventures come at a cost. Bobby takes a lot of unnecessary risks. For example, Bobby is quite the speed demon. He frequently goes over 90 mph just for the thrill of going fast. He's had several tickets, had his license suspended, and had even been in a few wrecks. Despite all of these occurrences, he still continues to speed.

He finds joy in doing other illegal activities like spray-painting buildings, sneaking into movie theaters, and occasionally grabbing a few candy bars from the convenience store without paying for them. There have been many times when Greg was with Bobby and got in trouble as a result of Bobby's negligent behavior.

Psychoanalysis:

On the onset, it seems that the Rebellious Soul's brain is wired for danger, risk, and adventure. While this is true, the further discovery shows that the rebellious soul is also wired for breaking the rules with no care for the cost of his or her actions. Where does this come from?

We can probably all remember a stage of rebellion while we were growing up. However most of us have learned that adults really can't act that way and still be considered responsible and mature. Rebellious Souls have probably gotten positive reinforcement for bad behavior that causes them to continue to act out. For instance, though their teacher may have punished her, the rebellious soul thought writing naughty words on the white board was worth it because all of her classmates laughed and encouraged her.

On the other hand, a Rebellious Soul may have been conditioned at home through parenting, or lack thereof. If

Bobby didn't get the attention that he craved from his dad as a child, he might have acted out in order to seek attention (He most likely didn't get the positive attention that he wanted through that action, and yet continued to rebel, creating a vicious cycle.) Once the brain is wired, it will continue to revert back to what it's been taught, until its rewired to act in another way. Bobby keeps rebelling to get attention as an adult from his friends, though he doesn't realize that there's another, less risky way.

While some may suggest that people are hard-wired to be rebellious (Which researchers do have data for), it is also good to know that rebellion is a part of our nurturing and growing up. When an adult is stuck in rebellion, it may be because psychologically they are still either rebelling against something or someone, or they are running from something or someone. If Bobby, as an adult, is still the rebellious soul who tries to get you into trouble, he may be running from the call to be a responsible and mature adult.

Additionally, some Rebellious souls have taught themselves through the repetition during their childhood and early adulthood that unruly behavior is fun or attention grabbing, and helps them make friends. Eventually, they will find out that most of their friends (unless they are also rebellious souls) desire grown-up relationships, not teenage rebellion.

What's the problem here?

Bobby is what I like to refer to as a Rebellious Soul. The Rebellious Soul is very fun to be around and tends to be the life of the party. This is a nice change from the previous two types. However, the Rebellious Soul is dangerous because they have no regard for the rules. They do what they want and have little care for the consequences of their actions.

For this reason, it is not wise to invest much time into a Rebellious Soul. More than likely, you will end up having a good time, but will also get yourself into a lot of trouble in the process. If you discover that you are dealing with a Rebellious Soul, here are a few tips on how you can manage the relationship.

Stay rational.

One of the biggest problems with the Rebellious Soul is that they have an invincibility complex. They think that they can do anything that they want and that there will be no consequences. Unfortunately, they could not be more wrong. Everything we do has consequences, so therefore it is important that you continue to be rational when hanging around with a Rebellious Soul.

Think about your actions before you act. If they suggest sneaking out of class early, stop and think: Is this a good idea? What could happen to me if I decided to do this? Always make sure you are thinking clearly about the situation before you do it. The Rebellious Soul is willing to take crazy risks and does not care about the cost because it is in their personality. Are you willing to do that?

Learn how to say no.

Although not always seen as the "polite" thing to do, it is the most logical. When the Rebellious Soul comes to you with a crazy request, it is perfectly okay to tell them no. If they truly value your companionship, then they will respect your wishes. The toxic Rebellious Soul will try to change your mind. They will do everything in their power to make you follow them.

Do not give in. Remember, this is your life we are talking about. You do not want to mess it up because one person gave you a crazy idea and you went along with it. If saying no does not work, then revert to the previous tip.

Give them other options.

Mainly, you want to divert their attention to something else so that they will not want to do the extreme action anymore. For example, let's say that Bobby wants to go into an old construction zone that is marked "no trespassing." At first, it sounds like it could be interesting, but then Greg remembers that there is a fine for trespassing the property. He could suggest to Bobby to visit a haunted house or some other type of building that is not marked "no trespassing." Instead of directly telling Bobby no, Greg only suggested something similar that was not quite as risky.

Conversing with a Rebellious Soul

Conversing with a rebellious soul is quite normal until the moments in which you have to stick to your values instead of following along with their shenanigans. Here are a couple of ideas on how to do that.

First - Talk about your core values. If you are trying to remain friends with this person, they should verbally hear from you what you value so that they are aware of when they are pulling you into a rebellion. This isn't a fix-all. A Rebellious Soul is going to continue to do "fun" things that are risky, however, at least you've let them know the areas in which you don't feel comfortable crossing the line.

Second - Ask them about their core values. If you are trying to help them to be less rebellious, you should spend time conversing with them about what they think they value. If you are at work or school, and your Rebellious Soul is thinking about doing something controversial, ask them if that violates anything that they believe in. For example, you could say something like this: "Ken, I know you're thinking about skipping class all week and taking a road trip. Don't you think that might hurt your grades this semester since we have mid-terms that week?" If Ken values his grades (or what a degree will get him after he graduates), he will rethink skipping classes. If not, you can at least revert back to reminding him that you do value passing your classes so that you can graduate and get a good job. Then it's out of your hands.

Third - Stay Strong. In conversations where you are feeling pressured by a Rebellious Soul, stay strong and speak confidently to him or her. Like mentioned above, you can use distractions to avoid yourself being sucked into their rebellion. Talk about something else, so their focus is drawn away from the temptation to rebel. When conversing with him or her, show them good examples to follow and how that would benefit them. While the Rebellious Soul loves fun and doesn't care about the cost, you can show them that they can have fun without any dangerous cost, and can better benefit themselves since they won't be getting into trouble or getting fined or getting fired.

Approaching Conflict - If you are in some sort of relationship with a rebellious soul, you won't be able to avoid conflict, unless you go along with all of their ideas (I guess you won't unless you like the idea of getting in trouble like a rebelling teenager.). Here are some suggestions when confronting the Rebellious Soul.

- Don't give them an ultimatum unless you have to do so. Rebellious Souls are… rebellious. If you tell them that if they don't change, you're going to stop being friends with them, they will act like they don't care. In fact, they'll probably go find someone else to be friends with them. That may be what you need if they are a bad influence, but that didn't resolve any conflict, and if you have to see this person on a regular basis it will be worse for you.

- Ask them why they do what they do. See what their reasoning is. You may not get a very good answer, but it will open the door to talk about why *you* do what you do, and why you choose not to do certain things that you would consider rebellious.

- Ask for something small. If you have a conflict with a Rebellious Soul, especially if you work together, ask if they can focus on one area. For instance, you could request that they concentrate on not skipping the weekly mandatory meeting since it hurts the whole team. That way, hopefully, you can encourage them as they do that small thing, and they may be willing to improve more over time.

Keep in mind that you don't have to be friends with a toxic Rebellious Soul. However, it is good to know how to manage to converse with one, if you regularly come in contact with one or if you are trying to navigate a friendship with one.

Wrap Up

The Rebellious Soul can be fun to be around; you just have to be sure that the fun does not cost you your sanity, safety, freedom, or your life. These are a few quick ways to identify a Rebellious Soul:

- Has a big problem with authority
- Constantly seeks to do adventurous, dangerous, or illegal things

- Has no regard for the consequences of their actions
- Does not care about who they bring with them on their adventures or what happens to these people

"You are only going to be as good as the people you surround yourself with, so be brave enough to let go of those who keep weighing you down."

-Deb Thompson

The Opportunist

Roger is among one of the top-selling associates at his insurance firm. Clients love him; he gets along well with his coworkers, and the supervisors say he is easy to work with. He has only been with his current company for six months and is already on his way to getting a promotion. His success does not go unnoticed.

Hank has been watching Roger ever since he first arrived. At first, Hank did not say a word to Roger. In fact, he acted like Roger did not exist except when he was forced to interact with him during staff meetings. However, after Roger started receiving a lot of attention at work, Hank began to act differently towards him. Now he speaks to Roger every time he sees him. He makes an effort to invite Roger to lunch. Hank even comes to Roger's desk periodically throughout the day just to make polite conversation. Interestingly enough, most of Hank's conversations with Roger consist of discussing what was Roger's secret to doing so well with sales and what he would do for Hank if he were to get the promotion that seemed to be coming Roger's way.

Although Roger was flattered by his new friend, he could not help but wonder whether or not his intentions were integral.

Psychoanalysis:

The Opportunist is charming but manipulative. Some of this trait could come from their natural personality. Though it is changeable, people with a Choleric or Type A personality may be more likely to be opportunistic. They see what they want and capitalize on anything and anyone they can to get it. They are headstrong, like to be in the lead, and plan on getting whatever they have set their sights on. However, they can.

Outside of personality, an Opportunist has probably grown up learning that he or she has to take care of herself and make his or her own luck. An Opportunist may have events in her past that link subconsciously to taking care of herself without regard for who she's using along the way. Hank grew up in a household in which he didn't have much to call his own. He had to work for everything and was taught to fend for himself using any means possible. His parents wanted better for him and encouraged him to be successful in life. Hank didn't want to let his parents down, and throughout his childhood, he learned to figure out clever ways to get what he wanted or needed to be successful.

Now, as an adult, Hank doesn't stop his opportunistic ways. When he talks smoothly and compliments, he gets people to like him. When he gets people to like him, he gets what he wants – whether at the workplace or in his personal life. When he gets what he wants, he feels happy and satisfied, better than how he felt while he was growing up. The Opportunist may have a hard past, but that does not allow for their manipulative behavior in the present. Their brain is wired to do whatever it takes to take care of self, without much regard for others. This is a recipe for disaster in any type of relationship, and you should not let yourself remain stuck in any kind of relationship with an opportunistic person.

What is the problem here?

Roger is someone that we all will encounter at some point in our lives: an Opportunist. The Opportunist is someone who comes around when there is an opportunity for them to benefit. They tend to be very friendly and helpful at first; but as soon as they get what they want, they vanish. The dangerous thing about Opportunists is that they tend to be very patient. In other words, they will wait years if they have to receive whatever benefit they believe that you possess.

Julie from the first chapter shows signs of being an Opportunist. She does not necessarily have to care about the man that she is dating. Instead, her goal was to reap as many benefits as possible from him. For her, the benefit was money, clothes, and jewelry. In the Roger and Hank situation, the benefit was an increase in sale volume along with the possibility of a higher position. Hank did not want to be friends with Roger until he saw that Roger could help him quickly reach a particular goal.

Unlike the previous toxic people that we have dealt with, you should never under any circumstances acquaint yourself with an opportunist. They will always have ill intentions, and there is nothing that you can do for that person. You should not try to reason with an Opportunist because they are simply too sneaky. They would try to find a way to twist things so that they will not appear to be what they truly are. I cannot stress enough how important it is to distance yourself from this type of toxic person.

However, just because you decide not to be friends with them, that does not mean that you will not be forced to come in contact with them. The workplace is probably one of the most common places to find one. For those situations, here are a few tips on dealing with the Opportunist.

Do not fall for their tricks.

Opportunists tend to be very smart and manipulative. That is what makes them so dangerous. They use their charm and intelligence to get anything out of you that they please. Stay on your toes. If you find yourself with a new friend when something good comes in your life, there is a good chance that you are dealing with an Opportunist.

The best thing to do is to keep a calm head and try not to let the attention to get to you. Always stop and think: what is the real reason that this person wants to be friends with me? Did you just get a big promotion, win the lottery, or buy season passes to a desirable sports team? Do not let the Opportunist charm their way into your life.

When you spot one, run.

If you clearly notice that someone is an Opportunist, do yourself a favor and leave him or her alone. Do not waste your time trying to bargain with them or even playing along as if you do not know what their true intentions are. The time that you spend interacting with an Opportunist can be spent with someone who cares about you and your well-being. Turn the other cheek, and just leave them alone.

Do not blow up.

There will be times when you come across an Opportunist who is very deceitful. They may even succeed in getting whatever it is that they want from you. Your first inclination will be to get even with them. Getting even may mean fighting, blackmailing, or getting revenge. Do not waste your energy. There comes a time in everyone's life when he or she realizes that their judgment was not clear and that someone tricked them into believing something that was untrue.

Instead of dwelling on it or beating yourself up about it, the best thing to do is to let it go. You're human. We all make mistakes, and we all have been tricked in some way, shape or form. Do not allow the Opportunist to have that power over you. Forgive them quickly, and move on with your life. What goes around comes around, and it is only a matter of time before the Opportunist reaps what he or she sows.

Conversing with an Opportunist

If you are friends with an opportunist, you will need to learn how to talk to them. If you don't need to be, don't be friends with such a person. They can't be trusted. However, here are some conversational tips for talking with an Opportunist.

First - When speaking to an opportunist, realize that they are using their words to benefit themselves and call them out. When you are conversing with an Opportunist, it's ok to question their motives out loud. For example, if you have a co-worker who didn't start talking to you until he realized that you're "in good" with your team supervisor, call them out on it. Say something light-hearted but truthful: "Hey James, we've never really talked much before you found out that Mark and I are friends. What's up with that, man?" When he answers, you can push him for more details. Be polite but persistent to find out what the Opportunist really wants from you.

Second - If you know that an Opportunist is only your friend to get something from you, make it clear to them that that's not going to happen (unless you're serious willing to allow them to do that to you, but this whole book is about standing up to toxic people...). Say something like this: "Look, I know that you are hoping to benefit from our friendship, but I don't like being used." You may end up with an Opportunist that has a change of heart, but if not, at least you've made things clear.

Third - Guard yourself against their tactics. When you are talking to an Opportunist, be on guard against their charm and charisma. Opportunists are deceptively friendly because they are trying to get something out of you. Be willing to be up front with them. Tell them "no" or tell them that you are only interested in friendships that go both ways. Find ways to let them know you're not going to be used by them, and be willing to speak it out loud (otherwise, they won't know).

This type of toxic person is one of the most dangerous because they are tricky and manipulative. That is why you need to be able to recognize an Opportunist when you see one, be able to talk to them without them taking advantage of you, and be able to remove them from your life when possible.

Approaching Conflict - This can be scary business. The Opportunist is magnificent with his words, and can quickly make you feel like everything is your fault, or can explain away whatever you thought the problem was. Don't allow them to trick you into backing down from confrontation. Here are some ways to go about peacefully confronting an Opportunist.

- Compliment them. Though they are not at all like Debbie Downers, is good to start with something positive when speaking to an Opportunist. They will start to let their guard down and may actually hear you out when you confront them instead of trying to spin it in a way that makes them look good, and you look bad. Find something good to say about them first, and then segway into what you really need to talk about.

- Ask what they honestly want out of the relationship. With a kind, unassuming words and body language, ask what the Opportunist is hoping to gain out of the relationship that the two of you share. If this is a romantic relationship, ask where they see the relationship going and what they are feeling. Do they realize what they are doing? Do they really want a lasting relationship? Similar questioning can be used for friendships and work relationships, to find out what the opportunist is seeking to gain. Knowing what their aim is may help in patching up conflict because you can either choose to work with them and help them by giving them what they want, or talk through why you're not going to give them what they want, which will establish boundaries for future situations.

- Have a third party there. This will help immensely in not getting turned around by what the Opportunist tries to insist is the truth. If you are confronting an employee who is using you, have another employee or supervisor there to validate both what you are saying and how the Opportunist responds. It never hurts to have a mediator step in, hear both sides of the conflict, and then help both parties to come to an agreement or conclusion.

Wrap Up

Opportunists can be very dangerous and should be completely avoided at all costs. This type of toxic person can be tricky, so take a moment to look at some of the ways to spot one:

- Only comes around when things are good

- Asks too many questions regarding how you achieved your new success
- Seemed to come out of nowhere, wanting to be your friend
- Spends very little time with you outside of a particular context
- Asks for materialistic items

"You can't change someone who doesn't see an issue in their actions."

-curiano.com (hongkidezu)

The Peter Pan

Heather is one of the most responsible people in her family. She was the oldest of her three sisters. So naturally, she grew up having a lot of responsibility. Her mother was single and worked two jobs, which left Heather to cook, clean, and make sure her sisters were taken care of. She didn't mind helping out, but she did not complain when her mother got married and had a stepfather to take on some of the responsibility.

Once Heather was older, she got a job at a clothing store where she met Frederick. Frederick was a good man and regularly came to the warehouse to keep Heather company. As time went on, Heather found herself catching feelings for Frederick and wanted to enter into a relationship. Once Frederick found out, he immediately jumped at the opportunity and even suggested that they move in together. It had only been a month, but she felt like she knew Frederick and was ready to take that step.

Less than a week after moving in together, Heather began to notice some things about Frederick. Firstly, she found out that he did not know how to cook. Therefore, Heather found herself preparing meals every day when she came home from work. Heather was frustrated, but she still said nothing. Secondly, she noticed that Frederick was always at the house. She came to find out that Frederick did not even have a job. His idea of working was playing Warcraft against other players on his gaming console all day to earn quick cash. This disturbed Heather, but still, she acted like everything was okay. Not only did he not have a job, he always suggested things for them to do as if he did have one. In other words, they would go out somewhere, and he would expect her to foot the bill. When she finally mustered the courage to ask him about it, he replied that he was used to someone else do things for him, and he was perfectly content with it. Because of her motherly instincts, Heather had been taking care of a grown man and didn't realize it.

Psychoanalysis:

Peter Pan has been trained not to do things for himself (or herself). Peter Pan grew up with a parent or sibling who took care of him and did things for him – from chores to homework, from spending money to laundry. This type of person's brain is wired to be happy and have fun, not to worry about being responsible or to really worry about anything.

Imagining Frederick as a child, he may have been the youngest child who had an older sibling who enjoyed caring for him. Maybe he had a sister with a caring personality. She didn't mind doing things for him. As they grew up, they joked about it, and even though sometimes she didn't like to, she felt like she needed to keep helping Frederick because it's what they'd both been conditioned to do. Frederick would ask for help on his writing because his sister was the better writer. She didn't mind because she felt good that she could help her younger brother out. It wasn't a bad thing – she was a good older sister. She didn't realize that she wasn't allowing Frederick to try, fail, and try again on his own.

Frederick didn't think anything of his childhood, but as an adult, he subconsciously searched for women who would take care of him as well. He is a sweet guy, but just never really learned how to make adult decisions. His focus is on having a good time and being happy.

They haven't matured because they weren't trained to do so. Peter Pan always had someone to bail her out. They don't have to worry about much in life, and always were able to focus on having fun. Peter Pan can't really help the way that he or she has been shaped by life. However, his or her brain must be trained to actually be responsible instead of being a child forever. While parenting strategies may be somewhat to blame, an adult who is acting this way needs to develop a mental strategy to break these bad habits and form a new, more responsible way of living.

So what's the problem here?

Frederick is a Peter Pan. If you are unfamiliar with the story, Peter Pan is a fictitious character that does not grow up. In fact, he is stuck as a child as long as he remains in a place called Neverland. Real world Peter Pans are very similar in that they have no desire to act mature, and their "Neverland" is all in their heads. The Peter Pan, like the Rebellious Soul, is quite fun to be around. They can come off as friendly and very personable.

However, they are people to be wary of. Peter Pans have the choice of growing up and living in the adult world, they just choose not to. They are immature, lack responsibility, and ultimately have no desire to do anything for themselves. They enjoy having others take care of them and make no attempt to do for themselves. If you find that you have befriended a Peter Pan, here are a few tips to help manage the relationship.

Do not give them what they want.

The easiest way to deal with a Peter Pan is to hit them where it hurts: their resources (or lack thereof). If you stop giving them the things that they want and stop taking care of them, then they will do one of two things:

1) They will find someone else to take care of them, or

2) They will do something themselves.

There is nothing worse than being used by someone that you care about, and Peter Pans will try if you allow them. Stop letting them use you. Vow to never give them what they want again.

Push them to do better.

There are times when a Peter Pan will not even know that they are a Peter Pan. If this happens to you, then you have to talk to them. Let them know that they have to grow up and take some responsibility because they will not be taken care of forever. If they do not have a job, make them get one. If they are living on your couch, start searching on Google for some rooms that they can rent. If they can't cook, direct them to Pinterest or get them a cookbook. In today's technological age, there is no excuse as to why someone who is able-bodied cannot make a decent living and take care of themselves.

At first, you may encounter some push back from your Peter Pan. After all, old habits do tend to die-hard. That is entirely reasonable. Don't get discouraged. It is important that you stay consistent and persistent. Revert to the first tip and vow to stop doing things for them. Continue to make suggestions on how they can improve themselves until you start to see results. Remember, you are the responsible one trying to help your friend or significant other to improve.

Kick them to the curb.

If you get to the point to where your Peter Pan just is not trying to do anything to grow up, it may be best to let them go. No, you are not considered a failure. No, you did not do anything wrong. It is important to keep in mind that the only sure fire way that someone can indeed change is if they need to change. They have to want it enough for themselves.

Just because you are friends with someone does not mean that it is you are obligated to get them on the right track. Sure, we would love to be the person to help someone grow up and be more responsible; realistically, that will not always be the case. At the end of the day, you do not need someone in your life that you are forced to take care of – not because they can't take care of themselves, but because they want you to.

Conversing with a Peter Pan

If you are friends with a Peter Pan and planning on continuing your relationship with him or her, you need to learn how to talk to them.

First - Be able to give them examples of their behavior. If you are frustrated with how they are acting – mooching off of you, acting immature, not caring about applying themselves to anything worthwhile – you need to tell them and give them specific examples so that they can see what they are really like. Some Peter Pans don't realize they are still acting like a kid at home. A meaningful couple of conversations with them may show them that they need to change.

Second - Speak to them like they are adults. Peter Pans are not really kids. Don't give into their mentality of immaturity and lack of responsibility. Say something like this, "Pete, I see that you still haven't cleaned your half of the dorm. I'm not your mom, and if you don't clean, I might have to call yours to kick your butt into gear."

Third - Be willing to have the hard conversations. With a Peter Pan, you have to be able to tell it like it is. This may not only include examples of behavior but imagine what their future will be like down the road if they don't change at all. Describe it for them, and continue to talk to them about their problem and ways to improve it.

Approaching Conflict - If you choose to keep on taking care of the Peter Pan in your life, and are happy doing it, you may never run into conflict. However, if you want the best life for yourself, I would highly suggest using these conversational ideas to confront them peacefully, and by doing so, to enrich your own life.

- Let them know it's not all their fault. Peter Pan may get defensive if you put all the blame solely on him. He may be unwilling to admit he has any kind of problem, or that there is any conflict between the two of you. Verbalize that you know it may be due to how they were raised, but also verbalize that we all need to learn how to be adults and do adult things.

- Point them in the right direction. They've never had to do things for themselves? Give them ideas on how to start. Talk to them about the areas they need to improve and help them find a way to get started. Peter Pans will be stubborn if it seems too hard to change. Why not just find someone else to take care of him or her and let him or her have his or her fun? Show them a simple way to get started, like washing their own dishes or making a checklist of their daily to-do list at work.

- Wash your hands of responsibility. This may sound harsh; however, you need to let them know, so that they know, that you are not responsible for them. If it is a roommate who's not doing their part, give them a timeline and clear desired improvement so that they know what's expected of them if you are going to continue living together. In any relationship with a Peter Pan, once you've done all these things to remove current conflict, future breaches determine increased action to be taken, such as having them move out or moving out of the relationship.

Remember, you are not bound to a Peter Pan for life. It is not your fault for how they grew up or for how they act now as an adult. If they are too toxic, it's not your job to sacrifice your happiness to try to change them. You can help them, but ultimately you need to do what is best for you on your own life journey.

Wrap Up

Essentially, Peter Pans are toxic because they are equivalent to a friendly leech. In other words, they are very nice, but they will suck you dry. They will drain you of your resources and even your sanity from the stress of having to take care of them. Let's recap some of the signs that you're dealing with a Peter Pan:

- Likes doing childish things like playing video games all day
- Allow others to take care of them
- No job or perceived way to take care of them

"People INSPIRE you, or they DRAIN you. Pick them wisely."

-Hans F. Hasen

The Stagnantician

Katie was part of a group of friends who had known each other since they were in middle school. They remained close during high school and vowed to stay in touch with each other regardless of where they ended up. Most of them had dreams of being doctors, lawyers, fitness instructors – all of them, that is, except Breanna. Breanna did not have a lot of drive, and she was perfectly content with working at Old Navy for the time being. She didn't know what she wanted to do, but she wasn't trying very hard to figure it out either.

After Katie had graduated from high school, she went to college, did well, and landed a job in her pharmacy field. She had succeeded in reaching one of her goals and was well on her way to working towards the next one. Now and then, Katie would go home and visit her old friends. All of them had gone on in their respective fields to try to make their dreams come true except for Breanna. Four years had passed, and Breanna was still working the same part-time position at Old Navy. She had moved out of her parent's house, but she still was doing the same thing that she was doing before Katie had left.

Psychoanalysis:

A stagnant person seems stuck in life. They don't have a forcible passion for anything really. This, psychoanalysts think, can come from a host of sources, most linked to past experiences. As the Stagnantician grew up, did they encounter a big decision that backfired on them? Did they encounter loss? Did someone in a relationship hurt them? Did they have a lot of change in their childhood? Did they get made fun of for having big dreams? All of these situations and others can cause a person to become stagnant in their life journey.

Think of Breanna as a child. Breanna was the middle child. Her older sister was determined and successful at everything she did. Her younger sister was spoiled and doted on. Breanna was in the middle, not the favorite child and not the successful child, just the middle child. When she was young, her family moved, and she had to leave everything that she knew. She was not good at making friends, and it took her a long time to feel comfortable in her new home, school, and town. She didn't want to go through all of that again, so she stuck around after graduating high school. She was never really pushed to do anything great, and though she wasn't coddled, she didn't have any high aspirations.

As an adult, this type of person will just continue along in whatever job that they got stuck in, with whatever friends they were able to make, seemingly ok with staying where they are at. Their brains haven't been wired to challenge themselves; in fact, their brains have been wired to stay with what's comfortable and safe. They don't ever really "do", they just talk about "doing". It's safer and requires less energy and skin in the game.

So what is the problem?

Unfortunately, Katie has been a friend with a Stagnantician. The Stagnantician, as the name implies, is a person who is stagnant or does not change. While there is nothing necessarily wrong with them personality-wise, they still have the potential to be very toxic to your life.

Are you familiar with the phrase, "choose your friends wisely because you will end up acting just like them"? The

Stagnantician is dangerous for that very reason. If you spend too much time with them, then there is a high probability that you can become just like them. Do not be fooled. This happens much more often than people realize.

Stagnanticians are the types of individuals that like to speak about what they are going to do, but they don't follow through. They are all talk. They will even go so far as to make fake plans on how they are going to do it. However, in the end, they never do anything. They continue living their lives in the same way and do nothing to change it.

Stagnanticians and Peter Pans may sound very similar. Both are friendly and personable. The fundamental difference between the two is that a stagnate person is more mature and already doing okay without using others; they just do not have any aspiration to do more. A Peter Pan is like a child: not doing anything and not wanting to do more. Both have the potential to be very toxic in relationships.

Here are a few things you can do to manage your relationship with a Stagnantician.

Do not follow their lead.

This is the most important tip of this entire section. If you decide to remain friends with a Stagnantician after identifying who they are, you must keep in mind that you do not want to be like them. There will be times when the Stagnantician's life looks simple. It's simple for a reason: there are not pushing to do any better. You do not want to end up regretting not reaching your goals when you had the chance.

Don't be sucked into the influence of the Statistician. Do not wait. Do not stop. Continue to push yourself to be successful. Do not allow yourself to become a Stagnantician.

Get them out of that mindset.

If you truly value your friendship, you can attempt to get your Stagnantician out of that inactive state of mind. Be honest with them. Start by explaining why it is important for them to want to do more with their life. Make sure you give them some of the benefits of moving forward, and also toss in a few cons to remaining the same for the rest of their life. Feel free to use yourself as an example if you have a success story.

If not, that's okay. Just be sure to explain all of the positive things that come out of your journey to achieving success. As tempting as it may be, do not tell them how hard your journey has been. It will only make them feel like what they are currently doing (nothing) is best.

Keep them at arm's length.

Much like the Peter Pan, you can't help someone who does not seek the help. When dealing with a Stagnantician, you may find it hard to get them to follow through on their plans. If this starts to cause you too much stress, do yourself a favor and be their friend from a distance. Never under any circumstances would you need a habitual Stagnantician in your life.

Conversing with a Stagnantician

While I don't think this is the most dangerous type of toxic person, they are one of the subtle and therefore can sneak into your realm of influence without you knowing. As you guard against becoming like your Stagnantician friend, here are some conversation cues for you to use on them.

First - Talk about the future. Stagnanticians are stuck in the past. While they may have moved out of their parents' home, in their mind they really haven't moved on to bigger and better things. They're fine just being where they are at in life and don't care about getting better. They are most likely to drag you into past accomplishments and stories and events. Talk about what's happening next, and encourage them to plan new accomplishments to shoot for.

Second - Influence them instead of letting them control you. Stagnanticians love to talk and never act. Speak to them about a goal you are currently striving to reach, or a task you are currently working on, or an example of something you planned and then actually did.

Third - Ask good questions. When they talk about things they will probably never do, ask them questions to specify what they want, or what they hope to accomplish, or what they plan to do. When you force them to answer questions, they have to think more about the actual task. Through questions, you can find out if they really even plan to do what they say, and maybe you can encourage them to actually finish what they say they're going to do. If not, at least you were willing to actively listen and help them.

Approaching Conflict - When it comes to a Stagnantician, even peaceful confrontation may be painful. This is because the Stagnantician doesn't like anything that stretches them, including conflict – even if it's healthy. Stagnanticians are avoiders. They avoid what could cause them pain or failure or anything negative. They think that sub-par is better than striving for better and possibly failing momentarily. Here are some suggestions when trying to confront a Stagnantician.

- Tell them what you want. If you are in a relationship with this type of person, the chances are that they say they're ok with everything. They are fine living an average life and are probably fine with the decisions that you make. However, that could lead to conflict if you want something worth striving after because they won't understand that or be able to support you in that. If you want to solve the dispute, you will have to be willing to share with them what you honestly want out of the relationship and out of life so that they understand why you feel the way that you do.

- Find out what they want. Funny enough, this may be harder to get out of them than you telling them what you want. They may be able to say a lot, but do they mean it? Talk about their real goals and dreams. If they really don't want anything out of life, you may need to consider leaving the relationship. If they can't be real with you and share what they desire deep down inside of themselves, then you may also need to consider leaving. But first, try to peacefully confront them about their feelings and desires.

- Don't let them ignore the problem. Stagnanticians are so okay with the mediocre that they feel safe in it; in fact, they will ignore things that cause waves in their lives. Ask them to commit to sitting down with you and have a conversation from start to finish to resolve the conflict between the two of you. Let them know that you are not pressuring them (They tend to not like pressure), and ask them to be willing to talk things out with you.

Don't get hung up on Stagnanticians. If you are friends with one, try to help them actualize what they say they are going to do, but don't put too much pressure on yourself. It's not your life, and it's not your responsibility to help them find drive within themselves. Worry about your own goals, dreams, and plans.

Wrap Up

Yes, Stagnanticians can be very friendly; however, the danger lies in letting them influence you. People do best when they are either at their full potential or are seeking to reach it. No good comes from being stagnant. Here is a quick recap of the characteristics of a Stagnantician.

- Has no drive to better them
- Content with mediocrity
- Talks about doing things, but never does them

"Boundaries are a part of self-care. They are healthy, normal, and necessary."

-Doreen Virtue

The Freeloader

Jake worked as a full-time employee at JC Penny. He had been working at the same location for several years. He saw people come and go all the time, but he still managed to hold on to his position as a supervisor. Recently, a new guy named Billy got hired. Billy had excellent credentials on his resume. He had been the lead in many of his jobs and seemed to be a real team player. Jake saw him as the perfect addition to the team.

At first, things went well with Billy. He showed up, did his job, and kept out of drama. Many times, Billy would even make it his business to tell Jake about the different tasks that he and his team completed together. Billy was well on his way to becoming an integral part of the company. Little did Jake know, Billy was not quite as team-oriented as he made himself out to be. Come to find out, Billy had been doing very little to help his team finish their work. In fact, his team members even said that he spent the majority of his shift playing on his phone or talking to others instead of doing the work. Jake was dumbfounded.

Billy would speak as if he had been doing the majority of the work and carrying his team; however, he was doing the least amount of work of all.

Psycho-analysis:

Recent studies show that bad parenting has caused some of the freeloaders that we deal with. While I won't stand behind that being the sole purpose of freeloaders, I will say that it plays a part in it. Children should be taught how to do things for themselves. If they are not taught to do their own work and to do a good job, they will push off work to someone else when they get into the workplace. If they are not corrected and taught to do better when they do poorly, they won't learn to strive to improve. You have to learn hard work somewhere. Your childhood home is the best place to learn it before you're a grown adult.

Additionally, some people may be more inclined than others to be a Freeloader, like someone who's had an easy upbringing and has had everything is done for them (Similar to Peter Pan). This can be proved as well. It's possible that Billy grew up in a home where he was taken care of and had everything he needed and got anything he wanted. He wasn't necessarily spoiled, but he was well taken care of. His mom was always home, so she took care of all the chores and also enjoyed helping Billy with his school projects, though Billy took all of the credit for it. His dad wanted him to have a better childhood than he did, so he always gave him money to spend with his friends. Billy played sports, so his parents didn't make him do any extra chores or get a job in high school so that he could focus on his sports. They also paid for the best training, but Billy tended to take all the credit for himself. Unfortunately, this trained Billy's brain to think that people would always take care of him and that he deserved to be taken care of.

As an adult, he thought he deserved to take credit for things that got done, even if he wasn't the one who did the hard work. Even though it may not be entirely their own fault, it's also not your fault that they are a Freeloader. Freeloaders need to retrain their brains to want to work for their reward instead of to steal it from other hard workers. While you can encourage them, you can't let yourself be bogged down by them. There are a lot of books, podcasts, articles, and etc. that help people to improve in this area.

What's the problem here?

Unfortunately, Jake found himself dealing with another type of person who is often found in the workplace: The Freeloader. The Freeloader is someone who has a habit of taking credit for doing someone else's work. They tend to try to blend in with everyone else and keep a low profile so that their lack of participation can go unnoticed. They are excellent at appearing busy; in reality, they aren't doing anything.

The fatal flaw of the Freeloader is that they seek attention or praise, so they will always brag about the things that they did even if they were not the ones who actually did them. Because of this flaw, they will always get discovered; it just may take a longer time for some. Using Billy as an example, you can see how a person can appear to be helpful and valuable, yet they rely on others to do the real work. More than likely, his impressive resume was the result of someone else's hard work that he took the credit for.

Most of the time, they are aware of the fact that they are doing this. In rare instances will it be unintentional. Regardless, these are not the kind of people that you want to have long-lasting relationships with. If you discover that you have been forced to associate with a Freeloader, here are a few tips you can use to help manage the relationship.

Force them to do the work.

This is the most important thing you can do when you are dealing with a Freeloader. The biggest problem with these kinds of people happens to also be the easiest to solve: make them do some work. Do not give them the opportunity to take advantage of you or the people around them anymore. Be warned: they will try to revert to their freeloading ways and fall into the background when there is work to do. Hold them accountable for everything that they do, so that there will be no way that they can lie about it. If you are in a management position, this should be easy to do. If you're not, then go straight to the next tip.

Take credit for what you do.

Many people find a slight problem with doing this. They believe that their work should speak for itself and that there is no need to tell others what they did. Do yourself a favor and get that perfect world that you are dreaming about out of your head. More often than not, people are not given the proper credit for the things that they do. Whether it is from modesty, lack of communication, or something else of that nature, people allow their accomplishments to go unvalued. This is the perfect place for the Freeloader to sweep in and take false credit.

If you want to get what you truly deserve, then you have to not only work for it but also showcase it in a respectable way. This is not to be confused with bragging. Instead, think of it as letting others know that you have completed your job, particularly your supervisors. Do not just sit back and allow someone else to reap the rewards of your hard work.

Refuse to do their work.
This one may be tricky. You do not want to jeopardize your job just to teach someone a lesson. You have to do this in a way that will expose the Freeloader for who they

are. For example, if you worked in a clothing store, then you can devise a plan with your other coworkers to make sure that all the work gets done except for what the Freeloader is supposed to do. If you work in a more corporate environment, make sure that you intentionally "forget" to accomplish one of the assignments listed. As long as you do some of the work, but not all of it, you have a better chance of proving to your boss how unhelpful the Freeloader truly is.

Conversing with a Freeloader

If you are dealing with a Freeloader, you probably don't want them in your life. They are an easier toxic person to be willing to get rid of. Here are some ideas for when you are conversing with such a person.

First - Be blunt with them. If you work with a freeloader, talk to them bluntly; they don't deserve your sensitivity. If they are not doing their job, confront them about it. The worst thing to do is not say anything at all, and then they just get away with it. You are both adults, so say something like this: "Hey Michelle, the rest of the team would appreciate it if you did your own work. We all have lives outside of the office, and no one here is planning on picking up your slack."

Second - If you see them starting to do something right, notice it with your words. If a Freeloader is starting to take steps towards changed behavior, notice it and make a big deal about it. Tell them how much better it is to have everyone do their share. Tell your supervisor to acknowledge it. Do what you can to get that sort of right behavior repeated in the future.

Third - If it's outside of the workplace, be up front with your friend about not covering for them. If they are always using you without putting in any effort, let them know that that's not going to fly, or that you may have to stop being friends. As with many of the other toxic people, you have to be willing, to be honest with them, or you can't expect any type of change.

Approaching Conflict - When approaching conflict with a Freeloader, you will need to be prepared to hear explanations, excuses, and maybe even lies. Freeloaders don't like to be called out for what they've done, or haven't done. Here are some tips on how to have a peaceful confrontation with them.

- Know the facts and be prepared to show them. If you are working with a freeloader and need to confront them about how they are taking credit for your work or for someone else's work, know the facts of what happened and have a way to show what happened. If you can (nicely) prove to them that you know what they're up to, they will be aware that they won't be able to keep getting away with it. Let them know that it's not ok, but that you want to work with them to build a better work relationship. In other relationships, the same applies. They need to know that it's not ok to be a freeloader, but that you're willing to give them another shot if they're willing to change.

- Have someone back you up. If someone else was a part of the situation, have him or her there to validate what you're saying and to be a third party mediator. This person can help if the freeloader is refusing to admit he or she did anything against you. They can also help with the next tip, setting up a plan so that it won't happen again.

- Talk through a plan to improve. If this person really wants to be a part of your life or wants to keep his or her job, then they need a plan to improve. How can you help with that? It's not your responsibility, but you can be willing to hold them accountable if they are willing to set up a plan to do their own work or not take credit for anything anyone else does.

When conversing with a freeloader, let them know that you know what they're doing, and that you're not ok with it and that you're not going to cover for them. If need be, let them know that you'll be taking the conflict to your superior (or in family situations, to a third party).

Wrap Up

Freeloaders are toxic because they cause us to experience higher levels of stress. They make us question our value and make us work harder than what is necessary to pick up their slack. Do not surround yourself with Freeloaders. The following is a quick recap of some of the signs that you may have a Freeloader in your circle:

- Brags to supervisors about the things they didn't actually do
- Claims to be a leader, but coworkers say otherwise
- Are nowhere to be found when the real work has to be done

"Knowing when to walk away is wisdom. Being able to stay is courage. Walking away with your head held high is dignity."

-angelstyle

The IYB

Kelly just moved to a new city. She is a little shy, so she was having trouble meeting people and making new friends. One day while she was at the coffee shop, she answered a phone call from her mother. After talking to her for a minute, she hung up, and another woman walked up to her. She had noticed Kelly at the shop a few times and introduced herself as Betty. Betty was very outgoing and friendly: exactly what Kelly thought she needed to get her social life started in her new environment.

For a while, everything was great. Kelly was spending more and more time with Betty. Betty was very curious about Kelly. She wanted to know any and everything about her, especially the bad things. As time went on, Kelly started to notice a few things. For one thing, Betty was always talking about someone else. It was as if she could not function properly if she were not seeking information about other people or talking about them. On top of that, she was not saying nice things about these people. The weirdest thing about the situation: she acted entirely differently when she got around them. She would laugh and smile in their faces as if they were the best of friends. Then, once she and Kelly left them, Betty would start making comments about them. It made Kelly start to wonder: what did Betty say about her when she wasn't around?

Psychoanalysis:

The psychoanalysis of an IYB (In Your Business) shows that the IYB is in one of two general categories: either they are hiding their own secrets behind everyone else's stories, or they have never been taught personal boundaries. An IYB who is always in everyone else's business, but never shares their own is most likely hiding their own life drama that they don't want to face or be vulnerable about. Such a person has wired their brain to cover up for their vulnerabilities by hearing and sharing the weaknesses of others. An IYB who never learned etiquette about how to talk to people and when to share or not share is not trust-worthy and is worth avoiding.

Growing up, the IYB person ingrained into their brain that when they have the dirt on everyone else, they wouldn't be the one to get hurt. They also found out that gossiping gains fake friends, which to he or she felt better than no friends. This person, like Betty, could have had a childhood in which they were not the prettiest, strongest, skinniest, funniest, smartest, or most athletic. They had to find a way to be the best at something. So they became the best at knowing things. These people like to be in everyone's business, knowing the latest news on everyone and spreading it. Once trained, such a brain will continue in similar actions into adulthood so that they can do well in the work world or in their personal life.

Either of these two types has most likely learned from past experiences that they make friends by sharing information. They feel more confident of themselves when they have all of these "friends", though they are most likely not real friends. What the IYB doesn't realize, for some reason, is that they don't have real friends, and their lifestyle is toxic. This can be changed, but it will take the IYB focusing on his or her words and conversational tactics. It's not your job to change them.

What's the problem here?

Kelly has sadly been a victim of befriending what we will call the IYB. IYB stands for In Your Business. As the name implies, the IYB is a person that is the equivalent of the modern day busy body. They spend the majority of their time with either talking about other people or trying to find out information about others. They always want to know what's going on with everyone at all times. To be blunt: they are nosey gossips.

The biggest reason why the IYB is so bad for you is that they do not have kind intentions. Sure, they may come off as being kind. However, they do the same thing to people that they talk about as well. The problem is that it is impossible to tell whether or not they are your friends. The best thing to do is to steer clear of them altogether and save yourself a headache. If that isn't an option, here are a few things you can do to help manage your relationship with the IYB.

Don't tell them anything personal.

This is probably the easiest way to outwit your IYB. They thrive on learning about other people's business and having something to talk about. Don't give them the opportunity to make you the object of their peril. If you decide to remain friends with an IYB, keep them in what I would like to call a limited profile view. Think about how on Facebook you have the option of customizing what you allow everyone to see. Take this same approach when dealing with your IYB. Only tell them things that you would feel comfortable with the whole world knowing because chances are whatever you tell them will be exposed to everyone.

Learn to be the best listener in the world.

This tip makes sense if you stop telling them all of your personal business. If all you're doing is listening to them talk about everyone else, you do not have to worry about them trying to find things out about you. Essentially, you are going to act very similarly to a cliqued therapist. Smile and nod your head. Do much more listening than talking.

Again, the key is to give a little insight into your personal business as possible. If they try to pry into your happenings, which they will be prepared to deflect it. For example, if while talking about another friend, they ask you if you have ever done anything similar, do not tell them anything. Instead, ask them to tell you more or even to say something about themselves. The trick is to flip it in a way so that you never have to talk about yourself unless you choose to do so. Your only job is to listen.

Do not try to get even with them.

The most harmful thing you can do is to allow someone to get under your skin to the point that you are retaliating back at them. Don't allow this to happen. It is too easy to fall into the bad habits of the IYB. When you realize that the person you're dealing with is an IYB, simply do the first two tips mentioned here. You do not want to resort to violence or even stoop so far as to become an IYB yourself. Be the bigger person and manage the situation properly.

Conversing with an IYB

Conversing with an IYB can be difficult because they tend to lead conversations with their prying questions and sharing of gossip. Here are some thoughts on trying to take part in a conversation with the IYB.

First - Consider what you are saying to an IYB. They are 99% chance going to share it with someone else. You have to accept that and really think about what you want to be talking about with such a person.

Second - If you have to speak to an IYB, only share facts and information that need to be discussed. Keep to the point, especially when at work. They may try to ask you personal questions, or questions about others; don't bite. Stay strictly professional, and don't give them any ammunition to use against you or others. You don't have to be rude, but you do get to decide what you share with others and what you keep to yourself.

Third - Change the subject. They will want to know all the details about everything, and they will want to tell you the details about everything and everyone else. As often as possible, try to change the subject (if you truly desire to be friends with an IYB or have to talk to them for work or school). Keep the subject light and impersonal, or let the IYB talk about him or herself.

IYB's are hard to talk to because you can't really trust that what they're saying isn't just gossip, and you can't trust them not to turn around, and gossip about you and the conversation that you thought was just between the two of you. Don't get close to an IYB, and don't expect to have deep conversations with them.

Approaching Conflict - When planning to confront an IYB, be prepared for an argument. You don't want to have a heated disagreement; however, if they aren't willing, to be honest, and reasonable, you may need to call them out for what they are doing and then be done with them. Such a person can be very toxic to your own life. Here are a couple of ideas to get you started when approaching an IYB about the conflict.

- Give them a chance to explain their side of things. There is something behind why they are doing what they do. Give them an opportunity to share. It could be the first step in healing and improve. Additionally, it will help you to assess what you're feeling. If she gossiped about you, maybe she did so because she was jealous, and you could discuss that. If he is spreading rumors about co-workers, perhaps it is because he is nervous that he's going to get fired, and you could discuss that. Hearing them out is always a good place to start when dealing with an IYB person.

- Ask him to think about how he would feel if he were you. Have the IYB person take a minute to think about things from the other perspective. How would he or she feel if you were all up in his or her business and sharing it with others? Talk it through. Make him slow down and imagine the situation from the other point of view. Hopefully, you will gain their compassion, and bring their guard down so that you can talk about how to resolve the issue.

- Give them truthful grace without giving them ammunition. If she is sincere about changing, give her grace and move on. Take caution, though, to let them know the truth: no one likes an IYB, and no one trusts an IYB. By giving this person truth and grace, you will be able to walk away with a clear conscience, knowing that you didn't pass any ammunition for the IYB to talk about this situation and you behind your back.

That's all that you can really do, peacefully at least. IYB people can be hard to change, so don't consider yourself a failure if it goes poorly when you confront one, or if the

IYB doesn't change. In the end, you may need to remove yourself from this person's life entirely, if possible, if the conflict is going to continue to go unresolved.

Wrap Up

At the end of the day, as friendly and social as an IYB may seem, the stress that they cause makes them belong in the toxic category. If you have to spend a good bit of your relationship being insecure and wondering whether or not someone is our friend or just around you to know your personal business, then you do not need them.

Let's review some of the signs that you have IYB on your hands:

- Constantly asks you questions about yourself and says little about themselves in return
- Talks badly about everyone and seems to know everything that is going on with everyone
- Smiles on the faces of the people that they talk badly about

"Sometimes you have to unfollow people in real life."

-bossbabe

The Control Freak

Jasmine is a lovely young lady who has been living alone for several years. She works as a waitress at a small diner and meets a variety of different people on a regular basis. One day, as she was about to end her shift, she met a guy named Ken. Ken was a handsome fellow and dressed like a business person. Intrigued, Jasmine stayed a while longer and continued her conversation with her new friend.

About a week later, Ken convinced Jasmine to make their relationship official. In fact, he almost seemed to demand it. He even told Jasmine that she should move in with him so that they would have more time to spend together. Ken was a bit pushy, but Jasmine did not mind. She had been alone for so long that she welcomed the opportunity to have a companion. Like most new relationships, things seemed to be fine at first.

It did not take much time for Ken to begin showing his true colors. He made it his business to have a say in everything that went on in Jasmine's life, from the way that she wore her hair in the outfit that she picked out for work; Ken made sure that Jasmine did it his way. When they decided to go out in public, he would make sure that he made all the plans, right down to the food that they both ate. He had to be in control of everything at all times. Jasmine was unhappy, and she did not know if there was anything she could do to fix it.

Psychoanalysis:

Control Freaks are almost always perfectionists. Most likely, they are hiding a deep-seeded fear of their life falling to pieces behind that perfectionism. Their brains have been trained to hide fear behind the control. If they can control their life and everything (and everyone) in it, then they have nothing to be afraid of. However, little does the brain know that it's impossible to control it all.

This behavior may be due to a tumultuous childhood, where they weren't able to control what was happening to them. Ken had a family that was always moving around. His dad was in the military and was often on deployments. He had to move from school to school and didn't have much control over what happened to him. On top of that, he couldn't control the fact that his dad was killed overseas, and his mom had to work full time and try to take care of the family on her own. Ken felt at times that his life was falling apart. It wasn't fair. He was only a kid. He learned to do the only thing that he could do: control whatever he could so that he wouldn't be hurt anymore.

In Ken's mind, even as an adult, he thinks that the only way to be okay is by controlling everything that he possibly can. Then there will be nothing to be afraid of and nothing to be ruined by others. Unfortunately, even a Control Freak cannot control everything, so they try to control the small things that they can to avoid concentrating on past hurts or current anxieties. This won't solve all of their problems, and neither will you. Be careful of being in a close relationship with a Control Freak. Their fear often comes out as anger.

What's the problem here?

Jasmine has managed to get caught up with a Control Freak. The Control Freak is an individual who always has to have control over every situation. They are very assertive and do not like to take no for an answer. In fact, they will try to find a way to make it seem as if their way is the best way. The reason why the Control Freak is so toxic is that they limit your ability to be yourself. In other words, if you have someone controlling everything that you do, you lose a little bit if your uniqueness.

If you always succumb to what someone else says, then you aren't really living your own life. If you find yourself in a situation to where you have befriended a control freak, here are a few things that you can do to manage the relationship.

Stay as calm as possible.

The worst thing you can do is blow up on someone who always wants to be controlled. As soon as they start to lose that control, they get into an unstable state of mind. In other words, they may resort to violence or extreme levels of stress. You do not want to be around a Control Freak when they suddenly lose control of a situation. Instead of getting instantly defensive, take a deep breath and remain calm. Get your head together. You're going to need a clear mind for the next tip.

Politely suggest an alternative.

This is something that can be very tricky when dealing with a Control Freak. The majority of the time, when you attempt to change their mind, they will either ignore you, belittle your idea or just flat out say no. Again, do not get discouraged. Control Freaks may be difficult at times, but they are also human. If you suggest other options on a regular basis, the chances are that eventually, they will adopt one of your ideas. If not, then move straight to the next tip.

Be assertive.

There might be a situation in which the best thing to do is to fight fire with fire. If you are in a position where you are always being told what to do, then you have to put your foot down and stand up for yourself. There is no need to be rude or mean. Instead, just make it clear that you will no longer do what they tell you to do. Being assertive will help to gain the respect of the Control Freak and hopefully ease up their controlling ways.

Tell them that they are doing it.

Many times, Control Freaks have no idea that they are excessively controlling. They may feel like that are only giving the best advice or being proactive to ensure that everything runs smoothly. However, this is not the case with the more extreme Control Freaks. Take the time to tell them that their behavior bothers you and that you do not want them to tell you what to do all the time. They may accept it and work on improving the behavior. If they give you push back, revert to the first tip.

Essentially, being around a Control Freak has the potential to be quite frustrating because of the lack of individuality. Some autonomy and independence are nice now and then, and the Control Freak will try to take that right way from you. Although they can be great friends because they are so good at planning, you have to make sure to remain assertive when it comes to things that are important to you. You do not want to be in a situation where you have someone dictating your life to you.

Conversing with a Control Freak

First - Point out to them when they are being controlled. In many instances, they probably already know it, but you need to be willing to speak to them about the times that they are being controlled towards you. Talk to them immediately when they are controlling you in a way that you don't appreciate, and tell them why. When you do this, speak kindly, as speaking out in anger against a Control Freak will cause them to get upset, and they won't hear you out.

Second - Slow down. When a situation is happening in which you are feeling controlled, ask them to slow down so that you both can assess what is going on. If they are willing to do this, they are willing to change. Either way, it gives you both a chance to talk rationally instead of escalating a situation. Share what you are feeling and ask how they feel so that you can work through it.

Third - Hold your ground. Don't allow a Control Freak to tell you how to feel. They will want to control everything about you, including how you think, feel, and act towards them. Don't allow that to happen. Hold your ground and believe in what you think is right. Say something like this: "I want to be friends; however, I don't like how you try to control me. I have feelings and thoughts, and I can make decisions on my own. If you don't accept that, then I don't know if we can continue being friends."

A Control Freak can be scary to deal with. It can feel like they are always right and you have no right to disagree with them or share what you think and feel. That is not correct. If you feel that way in any of your relationships, you need to get out of them. If you have to converse with a Control Freak, use those aids to guide you, and try not to be alone with them if at all possible. They have less sway over you if you have another friend with you.

Approaching Conflict - It can seem unnerving to deal with confronting a control freak, especially if you are in a close relationship with him or her. You must be willing to be strong, or you will be controlled for the rest of your life. Even in a work scenario, you must be prepared to be confident in your case, so that you are not wrongfully controlled. Here are some points to aid you in confronting a control freak in a peaceful manner.

- Plan a time to talk. Control Freaks like to have as much planned out in advance as possible. Ask them ahead of time if there is a time that the two of you can sit down and talk. Don't blindside a Control Freak. Don't surprise them with the topic, either. Let him, or she knows that there is an issue that you would like to discuss and that you wanted to let him or her know ahead of time so that you could both think about it before you two sit down to talk. Let the Control Freak be a part of planning the time to talk. A Control Freak should appreciate this gesture.

- Take the emotion out of it. This is mostly for your own sake. The Control Freak can get out of hand when emotions are involved. She might be unwilling to see your side of the story because she doesn't know how she could be wrong, which will cause her to feel angry, stubborn, and indignant. For yourself, if you take the emotion out of it and try to be more objective, you will be able to hear him out and also share your side of the story without getting upset or hurt. It's ok to have feelings, but when dealing with a Control Freak, it's a good idea to discuss the conflict with as little emotion as possible so as not to escalate the matter.

- Be willing to put a pin in it, but don't allow it to be snuffed out. In some situations, you may need to allow him to put the conflict resolution on hold. He may not be willing to see how he was wrong about anything. In that case, ask him to contemplate on it and plan a time to talk about it again. If something like this happens, don't allow it to be dropped, if it truly is a conflict. A Control Freak is going to try to minimize anything that could be considered challenging to him or her. So don't let her sweep her wrongdoing under the rug. If she is controlling you, it needs to be talked about, even if it's little by little, so that it can be resolved.

Like many of the other toxic types, you may need to get another person involved when trying to confront a Control Freak. If you try talking and it doesn't work, don't keep putting up with toxic behavior. Get out of the relationship, if you can, or seek professional help for the situation.

Wrap up

As a recap, here are the things to look for when wondering if you're dealing with a Control Freak:

- Plans out every single detail to everything that they do

- Gets upset or angry when someone tries to change their plans
- Tells you what to do all the time
- Belittles everyone else's advice and tend to be very selfish

"When a toxic person can no longer control you, they will try to control how others see you. The misinformation will feel unfair, but stay above it, trusting that other people will eventually see the truth, just like you did."

-Jill Blakeway

The Habitual Liar

Tony is a partner at a law firm. He worked his way all the way from a paralegal to owning a share of the company. Tony's journey had not been very easy. He had to step over a lot of people along the way to get to his current position. Sadly, one thing that he got skilled at doing was stretching the truth.

One of his most memorable stories occurred when he was a big case with about four other people. Although it was not said aloud, everyone knew that whoever contributed the most to this instance was guaranteed their office at the end of the year. Since the vast majority of the employees were forced to sit in cubicles, the idea of having their office was very appealing. Each of them had a different responsibility and was told to reconvene in a week's time.

While everyone else was diligently working on completing his or her portion of the project, Tony had his plan. He started putting bugs in his co-worker's ears saying that this person was talking badly about that person, and that person was talking badly about this one. The rumors he spread were so believable that he made it impossible to be able to determine that they originated from him. Tony caused so much chaos that he made the other four people completely lose focus on what they were doing. As a result, Tony completed his assignment with flying colors—completely destroying his competition. When asked about how he didn't get caught up in a mess, he acted like he had no idea what anyone was talking about.

Psychoanalysis:

The Habitual Liar may not be officially diagnosed. However she or she has a trait can be linked to other disorders that are toxic, such as narcissism. A narcissist desires, above anything else, herself or himself. They are full of themselves; being blunt, they love themselves. If they don't think they're good enough for themselves, they will fake it, and that is where lying comes in.

Being fake may also be connected to a low self-esteem, which could originate from the childhood of the Habitual Liar. Tony grew up in a home in which the parenting strategy was strict. He got caught for everything, and there was a severe punishment for everything. He felt like he could never win. He wanted to be good, but he also was a kid who made mistakes. He felt like he failed his parents when he disobeyed. His parents never really showed him grace, he was an only child, and he was expected to follow the rules, no matter what. Tony figured out as a child that if he lied, he could get out of trouble. It's not the right thing to do, but since he didn't get caught, he didn't get taught that it was wrong. He started using lies to get out of hard situations, and it seemed to help him at the time. He might have gotten caught once or twice during his years as a child, but he found ways to lie better, and it became his initial instinct to avoid getting into trouble, even as an adult.

The Habitual Liar feels the need to lie to make he or she look better than others, or be funny, or get the job, etc. Unfortunately, lying is an easy habit to start, and helps avoid momentary conflicts; however, it is incredibly hard to break the habit, and so habitual liars don't even try to break it, they just continue on in the reality that they've built on their lies.

What's the problem here?

Tony is what we will refer to a Habitual Liar. With traits similar to the Opportunist, the Habitual Liar is the type of person who lies about everything and often for no apparent reason. They are skilled at stretching the truth in a way that will seem very believable, yet could not be more inaccurate. The primary reason that these people are so toxic is simple: they are not trustworthy. It 's hard to have a meaningful relationship with someone who lies to you or embellishes the truth on a regular basis. Although strongly advised against, there are some who would still choose to remain friends with a Habitual Liar. If this is you, continue to discover a few tips on what you can do to manage the relationship.

Try not to look too deeply into anything that they say.

These people are called Habitual Liars for a reason. There is a good chance that more than 75% of what comes out of their mouth is a lie. For this reason, you have to stay on your toes. As much as you want to believe them, don't expect them to tell you the whole truth. It's not you; it is just in their nature.

Question their information.

If you do think that you can remotely trust your Habitual Liar, throw them a curve ball, and question whatever it is that they tell you in response. Habitual Liars tend to be excellent at telling one lie. They rehearse it and get it ready before they start saying it. However, one thing that they tend not to repeat is to follow up questions to the lie. When you ask them a follow-up question, and they start to stammer, mumble, or even stutter, then chances are they are probably lying to you about something. Bravo if you can do this early on. It can save you a lot of time later.

Change the subject.

This one may seem a bit odd, but useful if you are having a continuous relationship with a Habitual Liar. Typically, once you discover that someone is a Habitual Liar, you get good at being able to determine when he or she are telling the truth. If while talking to them you discover that they are in fact lying, then you can simply ignore the lie. Although ignoring your problems is frowned upon, in some social situations, it can be acceptable. Calling someone out on his or her lies is not always worth the effort or a headache (or even their embarrassment). Instead of arguing with them, you can change the subject and act as if they never even said it. This tip can be particularly helpful in the workplace or at a family reunion with an annoying relative.

Conversing with a Habitual Liar

Watch out for Habitual Liars. Talking to them is difficult because you can't ever truly believe them. If you only deal with them on the surface level, it's ok to pass it off or ignore them. If you are trying to be friends or have to work together, you will have to at least strive towards honesty; otherwise, you will need to turn them to someone else who may be able to help them with their behavior. So how do you talk with them?

First - Call them out in a friendly (or not so friendly) way. It's not worth embarrassing them, as was just mentioned, however, there may be times when you feel you need to call them out. If it were just the two of you talking, that would be most ideal. You can just ask them to verify what they said because you thought that wasn't the case. That at least gives them a chance, to be honest.

Second - If you have to confront them because they've hurt you or your work environment or another area, do so calmly but forcefully. Let them know that lying is not ok and that they should find someone who can help them with that behavior (In some cases, it is classified a disorder, which is why it's smart to distance yourself from Habitual Liars).

Third - Reward honesty. Find honest remarks and stories and reward them, in your Habitual Liar and in others when you are in a group. Make a comment like this: "It's so refreshing to hear an honest opinion. I really appreciate your honesty in our friendship." Let them know that it does not matter to embellish stories to make them better, it's important, to be honest.

Approaching Conflict - Talking to a Habitual Liar about lying can be difficult. If you have a serious or recurring conflict with a Habitual Liar, seek third party help and get out of the relationship if you can. If you are planning to confront a Habitual Liar, here are a couple of ideas to help you.

- Create a safe place. Let this person know that it is a safe environment, to tell the truth. Habitual Liars can be afraid to get into trouble with friends, family, co-workers, etc.; though it doesn't seem like it, this person doesn't want to let people down, so they lie. Give them a chance to feel safe and know that they can tell the truth without being judged or punished for it, and then hold to that once you do hear the truth.

- Dig up the evidence. Whether you have a conflict with a Habitual Liar at work or in your personal life, find out the truth and have tangible evidence of it so that you can prove it. This isn't about proving you're right and he or she is wrong as much as it is about protecting yourself against a toxic person in the middle of the conflict. Find evidence of what you are confronting the Habitual Liar about so that you are prepared and so that you know you have the facts right.

- Know that confrontation may not work. The Habitual Liar hates conflict, so he will lie to get out of it. He doesn't like being confronted, and so he's already planned a lie to wiggle his way out of it. If you have to, call him out on it. If not, get out of the situation and the relationship. If it is a situation in which you can't get out of their lives completely, make other people aware of this person's toxicity and your need to stay away from him or her.

Tell the Habitual Liar that you want to make things work, but can't continue to be told lies. There are times in which peaceful confrontation is not going to solve the problem. That is not a failure on your part. You need to clear your life of toxic people and situations.

Wrap Up

Habitual Liars can be toxic if not checked properly. They have the potential to cause unnecessary drama in your life along with questions of insecurity. Do not allow yourself to become entangled with these kinds of people. Recognize the signs early, and either leave or manage the relationship appropriately. Here are a few things to look for when trying to identify a Habitual Liar:

- Tells "white lies" for no apparent reason

- Twitches or is jittery when talking to others
- Tends to "forget" important conversations

"The only way to win with a toxic person is not to play."

-Awakeningpeople.com

The Sociopath, the Psychopath, and the Narcissist

While each chapter has discussed a particular type of toxic person, these three will be combined as they bridge on disorders, and are therefore more serious and less common than the character above traits. Additionally, while information, advice, and practical tips will be given in this chapter, in short, it is more likely with these than any of the other toxic people that professional help will be needed in one form or another. Don't fret. If a person like this is in your life, you can still break free and live your life for you. However, it may take more prying, self-reflection, and healing than the other cases.

The Sociopath

Kenny is very antisocial. While being antisocial is not a disorder, he displays some concerning behavioral patterns. His friend Mary notices that Kenny doesn't really care about the emotional or physical well-being of others. In fact, he is reckless and impulsive and is not remorseful about violations he has made against others. When Mary talks to Kenny, she can't tell what the truth is and what is a lie. After talking to one of his only close friends, she finds out that as a child he was diagnosed with conduct disorder. Kenny struggles with alcoholism, which only seems to make matters worse. Mary is concerned about Kenny.

Psychoanalysis

Kenny is a non-diagnosed Sociopath. The Sociopath is extremely antisocial (Hence the term). This is a highly rare disorder, but when it is actually confirmed, it's hard to treat. This is doubled by the fact that people with this disorder wouldn't step out and ask for help. If you know a Sociopath or someone with such tendencies, you may describe him or her as being easily irritable and aggressive, and most likely irresponsible. You may say that they didn't have a conscience.

Where does this disorder come from? It seems that it is a mix of nature and nurture. An antisocial caregiver could have an extreme effect on a Sociopath's childhood. If a child was not naturally inclined to be social, and had a parent, who didn't show love or affection and didn't teach correct social behavior, that could result in an adult who was bred into being a Sociopath on accident. It is hard to determine how much of such a disorder is genetic and how much of it is conditioning from the child's environment. Either way, it is immensely difficult to reverse.

What's the Problem Here?

A Sociopath is dangerous to be in a relationship with. While you may feel sympathy for such a person, keep at the forefront of your mind your primary goal: taking care of you. That is not selfish. If you have a family member or close friend who you think may fall into this category, suggest that they see a specialist who can help them. It's not for you to diagnose. However, it is for you to figure out to what extent they will be in your life.

Give them a chance.

Everyone does deserve a chance to realize what they are and change. That's what you are doing right now, to the extent that you're not being abused or used. You realize what you are, what toxic waste you may need to remove, and what you want to be. It's ok to love someone who has a flaw. It is not ok to let them or their disorder rule over your life. If someone close to you is struggling with this, be willing to help them by guiding them to someone qualified to try to help them.

Know the consequences.

Are you working with a Sociopath? Is it your boss? Someone needs to be made aware of the situation so that you're not alone and you're not vulnerable to being hurt by that person. A boss who has no care for your feelings or you, in general, will not be a good manager. If he or she is not able to control behaviors or is impulsive in nature – as Sociopaths are – you could be in danger. Know that if you try to "fix" them on your own, or if you do nothing and allow their behavior, that you will pay for it.

Don't try to be the peacemaker.

Since they don't care for others and don't see that anything is wrong with them, they will not be easy to convince that they need help. They may even get secretive or paranoid as they don't know how to trust in general, and don't know how to trust you if you're saying that something is wrong with them. They have an unrealistic view of themselves and of life, and will probably lie to you, making it difficult to get anywhere with them. If you've given them a chance, that's enough. Advise them to seek help or get them help if you are very close to them. Then distance yourself as much as possible so that you are not stressed out and anxious about them.

Conversing with a Sociopath

If you are in a relationship with such a person, you will need to speak with them, however, keep in mind that they are irrational thinkers, have a strong habit of lying, and are rarely sincere.

First- Don't take it personally. If you are conversing with a Sociopath who is a parent, another family member, or co-worker, you may need to put up with them to some extent, especially if they haven't been officially diagnosed. So on a regular basis, don't take things personally (or seriously) from them. Check in with someone else who knows the person and the situation to double check stories or to vent about what they've said to you.

Second- Don't argue with them. Slightly different, not arguing with them will hopefully avoid unwanted drama. Sociopaths are pretty egocentric and don't have a capacity to love, so they will not care about getting into an argument. They will also very likely be dramatic. For instance, since they have a high tendency towards suicide threats, you may push them as far as that, though they rarely carry those threats to completion. Still, they don't have the insight or emotional reactions to having a meaningful argument with that would lead anywhere helpful.

Third- Don't give in to everything they say. I know those pieces of advice don't mix well. When dealing with a Sociopath, you need to find a very delicate balance between standing your ground and giving them points that don't matter in the big scheme of things. In all cases of dealing with a Sociopath, you should seek help from someone qualified to diagnose them and to give you concrete actions to take in order to help them and yourself.

Approaching Conflict- You will not be met with an easy battle if you choose to approach a conflict with a

Sociopath. As has been and will be repeated, these more serious toxic people need help. It will not bode well for you to try to fix them or your conflict on your own. Here are some practical steps to take when considering peacefully confronting a Sociopath:

- Consult your instincts. While I don't recommend trying to have it out with a Sociopath, no matter how well you think you know them, if you are going to confront them then you need to be aware of your gut instinct of how they are feeling and what that might induce them to do.

- Approach them with another person. Since Sociopaths take and do not give in a relationship, and are deceiving and manipulating, bring someone along as a mediator or as support for yourself. Have a friend to help you guard your heart and mind, especially if the Sociopath is someone extremely difficult to confront, such as your boss or a parent.

- Get professional help. If you have a conflict that you can't let go of or a Sociopath that you can't let go of (You should be realizing by now that whoever it is, you need to step away from their toxic lifestyle), you will find more success with professional help.

Sociopaths are dangerous people. What is most dangerous about them? They can somehow fly beneath the warning radar of most people. Though many of their negative qualities may stand out, people will try to fix them or will think they're the ones to blame, and no one will dig deep enough to find out what they are dealing with. Try to offer them help with someone who is qualified to do so, and back out of the picture, even if its hard. It will clear up your life and may even help them as well.

The Psychopath

Whitney portrayed herself as charming, witty, and intelligent to her co-workers. Gina liked Whitney for the most part; at least, she wished she could be more like her. However, the longer Gina worked for the same company as Whitney, the more Gina realized she never wanted to be like Whitney. Whitney was able to manipulate anyone to do anything. She easily moved up in the company and got others to do things for her. On top of that, she lied about everything and never showed an ounce of empathy or care for any of her co-workers. While Whitney must have learned to mimic normal behaviors, she would sometimes slip up during her deceptions. Gina also found out that Whitney would lie about keeping peoples' secrets to gain their trust and would tell them fake secrets in return. Gina doesn't trust Whitney, but she's not sure what the root of the problem is. Whitney comes across as a strong and confident co-worker to everyone on the surface. Underneath, she is a psychopath.

Psychoanalysis:

While the term Psychopath is usually now replaced with "anti-social personality disorder", we will continue with the simple phrase, though I'm sure the connotations in your mind have something to do with crime or murder, and very few of Psychopaths are actually serial killers.

The Psychopath is not normal for his or her behavior. To go deeper, breaking down the word to its origin in Greek,

Psycho-path literally means "mind-suffering". Sadly, research shows that such people have been much more conditioned by their environment and not as much by their genetics. It's nurture, not nature that has created the psychopaths in our history and in our society today. A person that has suffered horrible events in their childhood – such as extreme violence, negligence, and etc. – is more likely to demonstrate Psychopathic tendencies. The maltreatment that such children incur actually inhibit the development of the regions of the brain that govern emotions, leading to their actions and underdeveloped characteristics as adults.

At their best, Psychopaths can't be trusted from day to day, hour to hour, or even minute to minute. At their worst, they are a dangerous threat to themselves and others. They need to be directed to professional help, if not to reverse their disorder, then to at least assist them to navigate through their personality and their life.

What's the Problem here?

There is a serious problem here. Psychopaths are not able to feel remorseful or guilty. They lack empathy, and if they show emotion at all, they are very shallow emotion. Though they experience dysfunctional behavior, they aren't able to learn about it and change it. Some researchers are optimistic about finding a cure for this disorder, however, as of now, the best that can be done is diagnosis and treatment on a case-by-case basis. Treatment, meaning that professional help can aid them in living some kind of life; however, it won't be normal and shouldn't include you in it.

Diagnose.

I'm not saying that you're qualified to diagnose someone, but are you dealing with a Psychopath? As often as we flippantly throw around that term when someone seems a bit crazy, it could be detrimental for you to accuse someone of being a Psychopath when that is not their diagnosis. So how do you figure that out without their help? You could call a helpline or seek out more information about the specific signs of a Psychopath. You could talk with them or even suggest seeing a professional see what they advise. It is hard to be willing to consider serious disorders, especially if it is someone you love (like a parent or a spouse), but you are not doing yourself or that person any good if you continue living in anxiety and possibly fear.

A psychopath does not equal Serial Killer.

Studies show that only about 1 in 30,000 psychopaths are serial killers. Though they are not normal, many Psychopaths can get through life undetected by others or even by themselves. This doesn't mean that you take your chance with them and sweep everything they do under the rug. If they can't take responsibility for their actions, and if they can't talk about improving and show improvement, then they need outside influence, and you need out.

Forgive yourself.

Keep a record of everything, even conversations, so that you can look back and forgive yourself of the responsibility of the Psychopath's behavior. Document what you tried, what you said, what they responded with, what actions they took against you. You don't want to depress yourself, but you do want to be able to remember that you tried and that you were not in the wrong. They will try to manipulate you and make you feel like you're doing wrong by them; get them out of your head and forgive yourself. Hear this: if even the best of professionals do not have a fix for this mental disorder, you cannot expect yourself to fix the Psychopath in your life.

Conversing with a Psychopath

Good luck. Reflecting on what you've learned about Psychopaths, they are smooth-talking, charming, and slick on the outside. They don't seem to be self-conscious or quiet. They think they're the best thing since sliced bread, and they desire thrilling stimulation since they get bored easily. Somewhat under the surface, they are liars and manipulators who lack any affection, remorse, behavioral control, and empathy. They have no realistic long-term ideas for their lives. These are not people that you want to associate with or talk with on a regular basis. These are individuals who need help. Here are some tips if you find that you have this toxic person in your life.

First- Decide not to be in contact with them. If it is a co-worker or someone you see from time to time is a Psychopath, just decide not to be in touch with them. If it is someone who is closer to you, or in a position over you at work, ask for someone's help in observing them and deciding if they are a Psychopath and – if so – how to move forward. In any case, limit communication as much as possible so as not to be taken advantage of. Block them on social media platforms, email, phone, etc. The best choice is to not have conversations at all with this person if possible.

Second- Use other sources of communication. Instead of meeting one-on-one with someone who's tendency is towards violent behavior and aggressive speech, speak on the phone or through email. This way, you are not alone with such a person. However, even when not together physically, a Psychopath can manipulate and use you, so take care and tread carefully. As has been said, the real answer is to get help and to not be in situations in which you have to converse with a Psychopath on a regular basis, whether in person or in another mode. Write or talk to them in a direct way, and stick to the point, ignoring their schemes to make you feel bad or use you.

Third- Prepare to protect yourself. Psychopaths drain their victims in any way possible, including emotionally, physically, financially, and materially. When you are prepared for the worst – for verbal attacks, slandering responses, stubborn denial, and etc. – you may be able to at least get past them taking advantage of your emotional state. Speak to them kindly, but not softly, let them know you're confident and standing your ground (but not overly-aggressively).

Approaching Conflict- It is not suggested to try to peacefully confront a known Psychopath alone. They don't take responsibility for their actions and don't honor obligations or commitments. If you need to confront a Psychopath, it should probably be to talk to them about getting diagnosed. If they are resistant (that wouldn't be a surprise), you should have someone with you to back you up, and a secondary plan of stepping out of that toxic relationship. If you're approaching a conflict with such a person, think through the following advice.

- Get professional help. You can't know for sure that they are a Psychopath until they are professionally diagnosed. You can go to a psychiatrist first and describe what is happening and ask for advice. Additionally, if you've been in a relationship with a

Psychopath, you may want some personal counseling to reflect on your mental and emotional state, and to aid in moving forward with the Psychopath out of your life.

- Don't let them get inside of your head. If it is a parent, spouse, or other loved one, they will try to get in your head and make you feel like this whole conflict is your fault or is just imagined by you. I guarantee that they will use some method of shaming to try to make you think you are the one in the wrong. They will have you feeling like a bad son or daughter, or feeling like you wrongfully accused them. That's what they do. You can't let them get to you if you're really going to confront them. Know the facts and stick to them.

- Don't go alone. As has been mentioned, nothing good will come from trying to confront a Psychopath on your own. Bring someone along you can validate your story. This is significant if the Psychopath is your boss, as you may have a hard time arguing against what they are saying. In fact, others may be convinced that you are doing wrong. Do you have a trusted friend or family member who can vouch for your story? Who can prove that you're telling the truth? You need to have indisputable proof when confronting a Psychopath if you really choose to confront them.

Psychopaths are not safe people to have in your life. Whether they are officially diagnosed or not, they are living with a chronic mental disorder that results in violent social actions and reactions. Once you've detected it in someone, it needs to be addressed so that you don't have to be routinely talking to such a person. Even if it is a family member, action must be taken outside of your ability and influence, if they are to ever have a chance at normal life (It is very rare that a Psychopath is "healed"; still, they need help outside of what you can do for them). While you can make a guess at their diagnosis, only a professional can truly confirm it.

The Narcissist

James and Katherine have been dating for a year now. James is beginning to notice that Katherine somehow always twists James' words so that he is always wrong and she is always right. She thrives when he tells her everything that he likes about her. In fact, she can't get enough of his compliments. At first, he thought it was cute, and didn't mind complimenting her. Now, he feels like she is slightly obsessed with herself. She doesn't seem to care about what James thinks, what he likes, or what he feels. James is starting to wonder how he can get out of this relationship, because Katherine is somewhat controlling, and turns everything against him. He's not sure what to do.

Psychoanalysis:

Katherine is a Narcissist. The Narcissist is a like controlling Look-At-Me-er with a dominating personality. If you are in a relationship with such a person and want to continue sharing life with that person, he or she will need to be willing to get professional counseling or other help to learn about him or herself and change. The Narcissist tends to be overwhelmingly self-involved. You may describe such a person as being selfish, or vain about their abilities, looks, etc. Psychologists say that Narcissists desire admiration of themselves to fulfill erotic gratification.

Narcissism may trace back to childhood. However, it has been bred into the person as well. Thinking back, most – let's face it, all – kids are selfish at some point. However, as children grow up, they are (hopefully) taught empathy and to look outside of themselves. When empathy is not developed, narcissism could result. Perhaps honesty wasn't valued as important in the family, or self-esteem wasn't developed. There are many factors that build upon each other to create a Narcissist, but these are some of the typical childhood issues. This disorder is very resistant to being treated, and so a relationship with a Narcissist as an adult should be seriously reconsidered.

What's the Problem here?

Narcissists take and do not give. They are best at manipulating people and concentrate solely on their desires and needs. There are different forms of narcissism to identify a person. The two main types are commonly referred to as *Vulnerable* and *Invulnerable*.

Vulnerable Narcissists are what their name implies: naturally more sensitive, shy, and vulnerable. To mask their lack of self-confidence and doubt, they tend to hide behind another identity. They seek to feel good about themselves and are scared of rejection. Since they are emotionally unstable, they often use shaming, guilt-tripping, and other manipulating methods to get a reaction out of others.

Invulnerable Narcissists are what you would imagine as the extreme version of a selfish person. He or she is intensely confident in himself or herself and tends to be void of empathy. In other words, this person comes across as cold and unfeeling. You may describe such a person as thick-skinned, power-hungry, or egotistical. The invulnerable Narcissist believes that he is invincible, and he wants you to know it and gives the impression that he's better than everyone at everything.

Some Psychologists break these two categories each into sub-categories. While they may overlap and may not completely fit your Narcissist perfectly, they are generally accurate and are as follows.

The **Amorous Narcissist** measures his or her self-worth through sexual interactions. This person may manipulate another to get sexual gratifications, only to ditch the person and move on to another "challenge". They seem attractive, friendly, and even sweet, but they are only trying to please themselves.

The **Compensatory Narcissist** is all about hiding any past drama or bad experiences by heightening their current achievements and merits. This person seeks out weak individuals who will be an audience for him or her. Under the tough exterior is a weak interior that is afraid of criticism and failure.

The **Elitest Narcissist** is willing to do anything to succeed, including climbing over people and dominating any competition in their way. They tend to consider themselves better than anyone else and therefore feel entitled to special treatments in all areas of their lives. She is great at promoting herself and bragging about what she's good at. She will probably always be able to top whatever story or accomplishment you are sharing.

The **Malignant Narcissist** doesn't really care about what is moral and what is not moral. Additionally, they don't usually feel bad for any actions that had negative results. You may describe this person as being arrogant or as always having to be smarter than you. Due to their disregard for their behavior, as long as they are getting what they want (and what they think they deserve), this type of Narcissist is often known as someone who's been to or is in prison, or involved in something else against the law.

Conversing with a Narcissist

If you are conversing with a Narcissist, consider the following tips. Keep in mind that you will not change this person. However, if you have a parent or a boss or someone in your life that you can't remove that is a Narcissist, you may need these conversation tips.

First- Know what they are. Don't pretend he or she is anything but a Narcissist. If you falsely try to pretend that he or she is caring and loving to you, you will get burned.

Second- Tell them what they are. You don't necessarily have to be harsh, but you do need, to be honest. Ask him if he realizes how he is acting. Don't be surprised if he does. Narcissists are cold-hearted and uncaring almost to a fault (for sure to a fault, for they hurt everyone around them).

Third- Defend yourself against manipulation. She will manipulate you. Don't let her. If you have to converse with a co-worker or boss who is like this, you need to stand up for yourself because your Narcissistic boss won't care about your feelings. She may be so power-hungry that she is willing to make you look bad to make her look good.

Approaching Conflict- Trust your heart. Sounds cheesy, right? But this is essential when the Narcissist you are dealing with is someone close to you, as a parent. You may think in your head that it's not right to distance yourself from a narcissistic parent, or that it might hurt him or her. Deep down in your heart, you will probably know that you have to let him or she go out of your life, at least for a time. When you know that in your heart, you will find the words to speak it out of your mouth. Here are some practical conversational points:

- Pick your battles. Why? Because you will not win many against a Narcissist. If your dad is a narcissist, you may need to honestly avoid certain topics to keep any kind of peace. If it is someone at work or a friend that always has to one-up you, either let them or be selective about what you're going to argue about. It can get exhausting.

- Get more information. This is just the tip of the iceberg. If someone you care about has this disorder, you may need more information to approach them with a conflict. Also, get more information from your Narcissist. As with many of these toxic people, if you can find out why they do what they do, it may eliminate some conflict in places like your work environment. However, if you are always together at home, it may not be enough to simply understand them.

- Go to a specialist. If you are committed to working out the conflict, you may need to get a specialist involved. Go together to a counselor who can help you sort things out.

The Narcissist will seem to easily turn all fault on you. It doesn't matter if it is your dad, your boss, or your friend. They are in life for themselves and can't see outside of gratifying themselves and making themselves look good. In any case, in which it is possible, remove that toxic person from your daily experience.

Wrap Up

Sociopaths, psychopaths, and narcissists should be avoided at all costs. Yet many of us find ourselves chained to one through some level of relationship. This relationship status cannot keep you locked in such a dangerous and toxic situation. Seek help for your family member, friend, or partner who is exhibiting these traits. Seek help to possibly restore or at least resolve your relationship. Ask for help to get out of it (This will most likely be the case, at least until he or she has gotten mentally and emotionally healthier.). Don't stay in an abusive or draining relationship with a Sociopath, a Psychopath, or a Narcissist. In closing, here are some common signs that you may be dealing with a Sociopath, a Psychopath, or a Narcissist:

- Behaves amorally
- Avoids social situations
- Overly aggressive
- Self-centered and selfish
- Violently Aggressive
- Manipulative
- Lacks foresight for the future
- Lies pathologically
- Shows no empathy
- Struggles to show any emotion
- Irrational

"Closure happens right after you accept that letting go and moving on is more important than projecting a fantasy of how the relationship could have been."

-Sylvester McNutt

Show Those Toxic People Who're The Boss

I know I have just given you a broad overview of some of the most common toxic characters that you will ever come in contact. No one person fits perfectly into one category; this is not a cookie-cutter help book. The main idea to take from this book is that you are going to come into contact with a broad range of different people. Some of them will enter your life to help you and have your best interest at heart.

Unfortunately, there will be some who are only there to take something from you. This could be in the form of money, time, and connections... You have to be sure that you are always alert and prepared to deal with any of these people that come your way. It is easy to get discouraged and just give up on meeting new people altogether after reading this. That's not what this book is meant to do.

Instead, think of it as a weapon to use if you were to get caught up with a toxic person. Fill your daily life with positive encouragement, and clear it of negative influence. Toxic people poison your life. You need to do what you can to fight against negativity. Not sure how to do that? Here are some practical tactics to start taking control over who and what speaks into your life on a daily basis.

Unfollow them.

Unfollow toxic people, both on social media platforms and in person. Decide not to follow a "friend" who is toxic. You don't have to be friends with that person. This is particularly the case online or in apps. You can unfollow someone without he or she even having to know about it. You can choose to not have their complaining or lying or gossiping streaming your home page. While it may be harder in person, it is just as essential. You don't have to follow someone around because that person has a more dominating personality. You don't have to follow what he or she says to do or feel intimidated. You can choose to stop following such a person.

Unfriend them.

It's not required to keep being friends with someone because you've always been friends or because that person doesn't seem to see the problem that you do. Unfriend him. It's ok to be comfortable with yourself, without that toxicity in your life, and then to find a new, healthy friendship. Through technology, this is even easier. You can unfriend them without them even noticing. If they do notice, you may have to try to explain it to them, or you can choose to ignore them. At this point, they are toxic enough to you that you had to cut them out. You don't owe them an apology. If anything, they owe you one.

Block them.

In some instances, you may need to block someone from your life- in person or in media platforms. On social media, online communications, and apps, it is relatively easy to block someone. This is smart to do so that you are not harassed or stalked. In person, it is more complicated. It is best to have a good friend or family member who can help you in confronting the toxic person and in asking that person to leave you alone. In situations in which you are trapped, manipulated, or scared for your safety, you will need to get professional help. This book has not been written to give professional counseling advice, and it is necessary to get the help that you need to be able to live a free life.

Reconsider what you want.

Once you've cleared out the harmful gunk in your life, it's time to rethink what you want out of life.

Who are you?

Who do you want to be?

What was holding you back?

What makes you happy?

What are you passionate about?

Who inspires you?

Reconsider your life journey, now that the black toxic fog has lifted. See the possibilities. Think about what brings you joy. Decide where you want your life to take you.

Replace what you've thrown away.

In addition to reading this helpful book, you can find various encouraging quotes and inspirations online, through mediums such as Pinterest and Instagram. For example, I have included inspiring quotes found online at the end of each chapter. You can replace the junk that used to fill your social media and your mind with positive and encouraging messages. Find people or pages to follow that add value to your life instead of taking away value.

Once you clear your life of toxic people and their influence, you have to replace it with good. Especially if a toxic person used you, you would need to fill the void once they're gone. It sounds crazy, but you may find yourself missing that person, and you may even begin to forget why you needed that person out of your life. You deserve to be built up and supported. Find sources of peace, comfort, and empowerment.

Relax your mind, body, and spirit.

This is your life. The world is full of toxic people, but it is also full of life-giving people. Not every person is out to drag you down, and we are all battling flaws that we hope to overcome. Take a deep breath. Relax. You may be feeling overwhelmed at the thought of trying to deal with the amount of toxic waste in your life. It's not going to happen overnight. It will be a process. Knowing that you are taking the first step in the right direction should calm you. You can do it, one step at a time!

Show toxic people who're the boss: live your life for you.

You may not be able to get rid of every toxic person in your day-to-day living, but you are able to determine who you are going to let pour into your life. When you stand up for yourself and show toxic people you're not a mat to walk on, they will either choose to back off based on your words, or have to back off based on your actions. Live your life for yourself. You are the captain of your own ship, and you have the power to steer away from toxic people. Welcome to the real world. It's good, it's bad, and it's changeable. You can recreate your world, and you can enjoy your life journey. So, get to it!

"You cannot change the people around you, but you can change the people you CHOOSE to be around."

-SimplyStacie.com

Did you like my book? Join me for more books:

Luke Gregory on Amazon.com

CPSIA information can be obtained
at www.ICGtesting.com
Printed in the USA
LVHW012207290620
659290LV00009B/3181